Editor-in-Chief: Barrie Pitt
Editor: David Mason
Art Director: Sarah Kingham
Picture Editor: Robert Hunt
Designer: David Allen
Cover: Denis Piper
Photographic Research: Nan Shuttleworth
Cartographer: Richard Natkiel

Contents

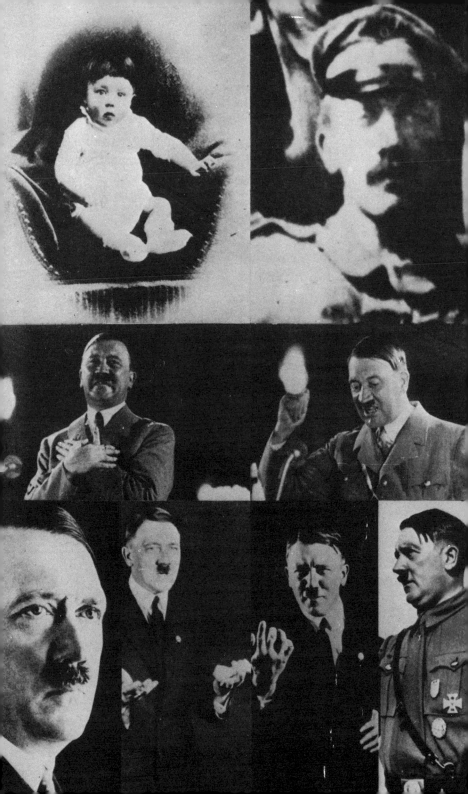

Der Führer

Introduction by Barrie Pitt

Not every reader will accept Alan Wykes' explanation of Hitler's behaviour as Party Leader and Dictator – which is that he had been infected in early manhood by syphilis and in later life succumbed to its tertiary effects: irrationality, irresponsibility and gross intemperance of speech and action. It is an explanation, nevertheless, which has been advanced before and to which the facts of his career will lend support. However, in the absence of documented evidence of this episode of his medical history – evidence which, as Alan Wykes makes clear, does not exist in a form which would stand up to judicial examination – the syphilis thesis must remain a thesis, albeit an arresting one.

Yet, the 'Vienna years', in which it is alleged Hitler contracted the disease, undoubtedly contain the key to much of his personality and destructive outlook. We now know that the story of a poverty stricken orphan's life which he propagated in *Mein Kampf* is largely a fabrication, and that the Austrian state, through the pension it paid him as the son of a civil servant, gave Hitler every chance to establish himself comfortably in life. He failed to do so because he squandered those means, and the dosshouse life to which he was reduced must accordingly be seen as one of his own choosing. For reasons all too readily understandable when the intensity of anti-Semitism in pre-war Vienna is recognised, Hitler blamed his lack of success and recognition principally on the Jews – not in any precisely formulated terms, for his mind never operated on precise lines, but in terms which laid upon the Jews responsibility for everything unpleasant, unjust and ill-organised

that he saw in the city and, by extension, experienced in his own life.

What roused Hitler from this self-imposed routine of emotional frustration and physical near-starvation was the Great War. He was intensely nationalistic (though not patriotic, of course, since he hated the Austrian Empire) and he eagerly accepted the chance this war offered him to cross the frontier and to join up in a German regiment. When the war ended, his record, his political outlook and ambitions and his very great natural talents were sufficient to launch him on the modest beginnings of a political career, under the sponsorship of the army. The relationship was to endure, though the army was to regret eventually that it had been entered into.

Hitler's relationships with individuals and with every organ and institution of German life have all been examined exhaustively. With none, however, was his relationship more critical than with the army. It gave him his start in politics and cast a protective cloak over his organis-

ation of the young Nazi party. It looked favourably on the Freikorps from which he drew so many of his earliest and most dedicated followers. But, as he was bitterly to discover, it would not brook attempts to seize power in the State without its specific approval. And hence it was bound to oppose Hitler's first attempt to make himself master of Germany – the Munich putsch of 1923. The lesson he learnt on 9th November, when his stormtroopers were shot down in the street by armed police, was one he never forgot: that in Germany, power belonged to whosoever commanded the army. Having failed to secure that command by force, Hitler spent the next few years securing it by ballot. Once attained, his earliest acts were directed to subordinating the army to his will and he did not rest in that aim until, in January 1942, he finally found the pretext to assume the office of Commander-in-Chief himself.

Given the obscurity of his background and hardships of his early life, it is hardly likely that Hitler could ever have felt much sympathy or liking for so unapologetically 'gentlemanly' a group as the German officer corps. Conflict between them was, indeed, inevitable, for their ideas on war were orthodox and Hitler's were not. Hence the shouting matches. The 'special effects' which went with the shouting – uncontrollable trembling, rolling of eyes and foaming at the mouth – might seem to lend support to the view that Hitler was the victim of chronic disease. However, those who knew Hitler from his Vienna days freely testify that such manifestations always accompanied his reactions to any persistent refutation of his views. He simply would not be contradicted, a habit which did not endear him to his comrades in the trenches later. It seems probable, therefore, that as Führer and Supreme Commander, when all outward constraints on his behaviour had been lifted, Hitler merely gave full rein to what was a natural trait. It always had its desired effect moreover. The generals blanched – and fell silent.

The victim

Those who set store by such things may care to know that the name Adolf derives from the two German words for 'noble wolf'. The family name Hitler is a variation of Hiedler and Hütler, both of which were borne by Adolf's forebears. Hiedler and Hütler have a tenuous association with the phrase 'guardian of the Gentiles' – which, considering Adolf's lifelong dedication to the hating and baiting of Jews, is not inappropriate, however fanciful.

There is unfortunately nothing fanciful about Adolf Hitler's existence. He began it on 20th April 1889 in a small hotel in Braunau, on the Austrian bank of the river Inn which divides Austria from Bavaria. Sixty-five miles to the west is Munich, the Bavarian capital, synonymous nowadays with the 'Peace in our time' conference at which the British Prime Minister, Neville Chamberlain, abjectly surrendered to Hitler on 29th September 1938. Sixty miles to the east is Linz, capital of Upper Austria, where Hitler went to school and ab-

sorbed the pan-Germanic notions that nourished his fanatical xenophobia.

Adolf's father, Alois Hitler, had neither phobias nor philias. He was a minor civil servant, a clerk in the Customs and Excise department. He was a man of middle size with a head as round as a cabbage. He had out-handlebarred Hindenburg – at that time a famously fashionable young officer in the War Ministry – in the length of his moustaches and was harmlessly vain of his achievement. A conscientious worker, he had been undeservedly hapless in his domestic affairs. His first wife had died childless; his second had died young leaving him two children to bring up; and his third – Adolf's mother – had given him four sons of whom three had died in infancy. Only Adolf and his sister Paula, plus the boy and girl of Alois' second marriage, had survived; and through the lens of hindsight one may

The infant Hitler. The first surviving picture, with newspaper announcement of his birth

8

J.F.Klinger

BRAUNAU
STADTGRABEN 318

The small hotel at Braunau in Austria where Hitler was born

have some harsh thoughts about fate's peculiar choices.

⋅ The Hitlers were Roman Catholics – though there is no evidence of special devoutness in the family – and Alois had to get a Papal Dispensation to marry Adolf's mother, Klara Pölzl, because her relationship to him of second cousin lay within the prohibited degrees of consanguinity. He was twenty-three years older than Klara when they were married in 1885; and when Adolf was six Alois retired from the Civil Service. In *Mein Kampf* Adolf says with characteristic pretentiousness that Alois 'bought a farm and tilled it himself'. What Alois in fact bought was a three-bedroomed house with a small garden in the village of Leonding, a mile or so from Linz. There he died in 1903.

Adolf Hitler was then fourteen an attending the secondary school i Linz. In *Mein Kampf* he is unforth coming about his schooldays; and tha is not surprising, for he could neve bear to reveal anything about himsel that didn't contribute something to composite picture of genius an nobility. He was in fact no grea shakes at anything at school. He had mediocre talent for drawing and go an occasional grudging 'good' for hi history and geography. But Augus Kubizek, who was his contemporar and who wrote a book *The Youn Hitler*, says that he was idle an unstable by nature, though 'he reall loved his mother. I swear to it befor God and man. I remember man occasions when he showed this love fo his mother most deeply and movingl during her last illness [she died c cancer in 1908]; he never spoke of hi mother but with deep affection. H

vas a good son . . . he always carried
his mother's portrait with him'.

Adolf was also affectionately in-
lined toward a girl called discreetly
by Kubizek 'Stefanie'. If we are to
believe Kubizek, Hitler was Stefanie's
love-lorn swain. She was considerably
above his social station and used to
drive daily along the Linz promenade
in a carriage with her mother. Hitler
stood on the sidewalk with his friends
and tried to ogle her. But 'from time
to time the two ladies were to be seen
in the company of young officers. Poor,
pallid youngsters like Adolf naturally
could not hope to cope with these
young lieutenants in their smart
uniforms . . . his anger, in the end, led
him into uncompromising enmity
toward the officer class as a whole, and
everything military in general. "Con-
ceited blockheads", he used to call
them. It annoyed him intensely that
Stefanie mixed with such idlers who,
he insisted, wore corsets and
used scent.'

He wrote countless love poems to
Stefanie, Kubizek tells us, and goes on
to describe one of them in which 'a
high-born damsel (none other than
Stefanie) in a dark blue flowing gown,
rode on a white steed over the
flowering meadows, her loose hair
falling in golden waves over her
shoulders. A clear spring sky was
above. Everything was pure radiant
joy. I can still see Adolf's face glowing
with fervent ecstasy and hear his voice
reciting those verses. Stefanie filled
his thoughts so completely that everything he said, or did, or planned for
the future, was centred round her.
With his growing estrangement from
his home, Stefanie gained more and
more influence over my friend, although he never spoke a word to her'.

Hitler's estrangement from his home
was caused by Alois's determination
to have his son enter the Civil Service
and Adolf's equal determination to
become a painter – which was, for him,
a way of saying he didn't want to work.
His tiny talent for drawing had become
greatly inflated in his own mind. He
says in *Mein Kampf* that when he
boldly told his father what he wanted
to do Alois replied, 'Artist! Not as
long as I live, never!' Looking at
Hitler's vapid water colours, which
are of about the same value to visual
art as is *In a Monastery Garden* to
music, one can't help feeling that
Alois' indignant discouragement was a
good thing, though it was a social indignation rather than an aesthetic one.

The estrangement became trans-
lated into terms of actual separation
after Alois died, but not for several
years. Adolf was too stupid and too
idle to pass his school-leaving examination and his mother kept him cos-
seted at home until she too died.

He had attempted to enter the
Vienna Academy of Fine Arts but was
unable to pass the entrance examination. 'Test drawing unsatisfactory',
the Classifications List of 1907 says
curtly. He tried again a year later and
was again turned down. Indignantly
he ranted about 'injustice' and forced
an interview with the Vice-chancellor.
He got short shrift there, being told
merely to try the School of Architecture since his drawings showed
marginally more talent in that direction. But the School of Architecture
refused his application because he
had no School Leaving Certificate.

Thus he was left high and dry with
no hope of becoming what he doubtless
saw himself to be – the Austrian
Michelangelo. In place of that lofty
achievement he developed a grudge
against the Academy's 'system'. It
was the first of many grudges that he
was to brood upon.

Bereft now of his mother, whose in-
dulgent cosseting had been like balm
on the wounds of his frustration, he
set off for Vienna, his self-pity turned
inside out so that he saw himself as a
conquering hero.

'With my clothes and linen packed in
a valise and with an indomitable re-
solution in my heart, I left for Vienna.
I hoped to forestall fate, as my father
had done some fifty years before. I was
determined to become "something",

itler's parents. *Left:* **Alois Hitler, a minor customs official.** *Above:* **His ird wife, Klara Pölzl**

ut certainly not a civil servant.'

He became, as we know, a conqueror f a sort – the bullying sort – and to iillions of the German people a hero oo; but for the time being he was othing but a roustabout – ill-clad, l-fed, and forced to live on such wits s he had. Rheinhold Hanisch, another oustabout who knew him in Vienna, ays that he wore an ancient black vercoat (a gift from a Jew named eumann) which reached below his nees, that his hair hung long over his ollar from under a greasy black owler hat, and that his thin face was overed with a black beard. 'Years of :udy and suffering in Vienna' is ie title of the relevant chapter in *ein Kampf,* but Hitler omits to iention that his study was limited o rehashing other men's ideas or iat his suffering was caused by is own idleness.

Neumann the Jew, Hanisch, a man illed Siegfried Loffner, and two others ppearing here as Stefan and Daniel ecause at the time of writing they are still alive and, for reasons that will appear in a moment, entitled to the privacy of pseudonyms, have all confirmed that Hitler lived as they did. They carried luggage, beat carpets, called cabs, washed dishes and scavenged round dustbins. Neumann and Hanisch acted as his 'art agents' for a time, accompanying him to shops and sometimes persuading the proprietors to commission posters and price tickets which Hitler would do on the spot; or persuading picture framers to put his sugary water colours in their windows where they occasionally sold to people who liked such things. (Hanisch's kindness was repaid by Hitler taking legal action against him for the embezzlement of part of a sum Hanisch got for a picture; and Hanisch was sent to prison for a week, the case having been proved.) That was the extent of Hitler's 'study and suffering' in Vienna. He had a great distaste for regular work, preferring to earn a little money and spend it frugally in cafés where he read newspapers and harangued the customers on politics.

He was a great bore with his continual sounding-off about injustices and inefficiencies in 'the system', his spouting of half digested information from indiscriminate reading, and his dotty ideas for acquiring fame. And like most manic-depressives he was always either sullen or exuberant, shattering everyone's peace with rantings against Jews, Habsburgs, Catholics or Social Democrats, or withdrawing into himself and refusing to say anything to anybody. He was a self-confessed cheat even before he left Linz. He told Hanisch that he had many times faked 'old masters' by painting pictures in oils and baking them in the oven so that they turned yellow and apparently ancient. And with considerable practice in cheap oratory he learned to cheat with words too, so that sloppy platitudes could be so spiced with paranoiac bitterness that they sounded like the trumpetings of a saviour of the German race.

The 'years of study and suffering in

Vienna' amounted in all to four. In 1913 he took himself off to Munich, where he hoped to fare better. But meanwhile something of great importance happened.

The lodgings, dosshouses, crypts, halls, cafés, parks and churches where Hitler stayed in Vienna are innumerable and for the most part untraceable. But one of them, at 27 Meldemannstrasse, is without doubt one of the places where the would-be saviour of the German race laid his weary head. It was situated in the XXth (northeast) District of the city, near the Danube, and it was euphemistically known as a 'Men's Home' though its status was no more than that of a dosshouse. The pseudonymous Stefan and Daniel stayed there with him; and it is from their testimony, made years later to the London venereologist Dr T Anwyl-Davies, that one can establish the facts.

Both Stefan and Daniel remember a bitter quarrel on an evening in April 1910. The quarrel was over a girl, a Jewish whore named Hannah, and it was caused by Hitler's having appropriated her to his own use when she was being paid by the others. Since Hitler was already indebted to Stefan and Daniel for such hospitality as their circumstances allowed, there was every justification for their reproach; and they were by no means reluctant to shower it upon him. They followed their home-truths with a good beating up. They pushed him into the dormitory, bashed him over the head and in the ribs, and flung him into the street. He screamed imprecations at them and by way of reply they flung his inks, pens, paints and brushes after him. That was the last they saw of him that night.

After an hour or so they both went out again, this time to find Hannah and bring her in from her beat. Her trade was mostly in doorways near the Nordwestbahnhof – a rapid but wearying trade sometimes involving four customers an hour (at fifty heller each, that is about threepence by 1910 values) and she no doubt found the dosshouse, with its lousy biscuit beds, comparatively comfortable and her customers Stefan and Daniel comparatively undemanding. They recall that she often stayed an hour or two (having bribed the janitor, who was the only person concerned with the No Women rule, with a few cigarettes on the way in) and then returned to her beat near the station.

On this particular evening they noticed that the faint rash they had seen on her body on the last occasion they had been with her had disappeared. She could hardly be called clean, but at least she no longer looked as if she had what they had thought might be heat rash or flea bites in the fading-out stage. It may seem naïve for two young men in their late teens and obviously promiscuous to suppose anything so innocent as flea bites on their consort; but although they had heard of venereal diseases their knowledge was vague. It certainly included nothing about the diseases' clinical manifestations and even if it had they were living, existing, rather – in a manner that would have left them indifferent. If they had known on that evening that they were already incubating in their bodies the germs of syphilis transferred from Hannah on the occasion of their previous intercourse they would have been maliciously heartened to know too that Hitler also had been corrupted – and on the very occasion for which they had been lambasting him. Knowing nothing, they satisfied themselves in turn with Hannah, gave her the hundred heller or so they could scrape up between them, and turned her loose.

Hitler returned to lodge at the dosshouse a week or two later. Stefan and Daniel took no exception to that: they had worked their indignation off by beating him up and couldn't be bothered to extend their enmity. But they observed that when he took off his clothes to have them de-loused by baking in the dosshouse oven, he, like

Adolf Hitler (back row, middle) and classmates at primary school. Despite the confident pose, his school career was undistinguished

Themselves, had a suspicion of a pink ash. They still didn't associate the ash with Hannah; nor did their general feeling of ill-being seem to them remarkable. They were not living the kind of life likely to encourage hundred per cent health; and then, after a while, the rash was accompanied by various other unpleasant manifestations they wisely went to a doctor, and on being told the alarming diagnosis of syphilis were maliciously comforted when they recalled that Hitler had exhibited the same rash. By now he was probably in the same unpleasant state that they were in. They accepted the treatment the doctor was able to give them, which at that time was an ointment compounded mainly of mercury, and wondered if Hitler too had had the sense to seek medical aid.

It seems to all intents and purposes certain that he did not – anyway not at that early stage of infection when treatment is vital. Felix Kersten, personal physician to Heinrich Himmler, the Gestapo chief, offers the soundest evidence that Hitler was irrevocably gripped by the disease. In his diary for 12th December 1942 he writes:

'This was the most exciting day I've had since I first began treating Himmler. (Kersten was a therapist who was able to relieve Himmler of pain caused by an internal illness.) He was very nervous and restless; I realized that he had something on his mind and questioned him about it. His reply was to ask me: "Can you treat a man suffering from severe headaches, dizziness and insomnia?"

'"Of course, but I must examine him before I can give a definite opinion," I answered. "Above all I must know the cause of these symptoms."

'Himmler replied: "I'll tell you who he is. But you must swear to tell no-

By 1944 Hitler was heavily dependent on the drugs and quackish remedies of Dr Morell, his personal physician

body about it and treat what I confide in you with the utmost secrecy."

'My answer was; that as a doctor, I was constantly having secrets entrusted to me; it was no new experience for me, as the strictest discretion was part of my professional duty.

'Himmler then fetched a black portfolio from his safe and took a blue manuscript from it, saying: "Read this. Here are the secret documents with the report on the Führer's illness."

'The report comprised twenty-six pages and at a first glance I realized that it had drawn freely on Hitler's medical record from the days when he lay blinded in a hospital at Pasewalk. From there the report went on to establish that in his youth as a soldier Hitler had fallen a victim to poison gas; he had been incompetently treated so that for a time he was in danger of blindness. There were also even in that early report, symptoms associated with syphilis. In 193 symptoms appeared which proved that syphilis was continuing its ravages and at the beginning of 1942 symptoms of a similar nature showed beyond any shadow of doubt that Hitler was suffering from progressive paralysis. Every symptom was present except for fixity of vision and confusion of speech.

'I handed the report back to Himmler and informed him that unfortunately I could do nothing in this case as my speciality was manual therapy, not venereal disease.

'He told me that Morell (Hitler's personal physician) was giving him injections and asserted that these would check the progress of the disease, and in any event maintain the Führer's ability to work.'

There is a good deal of more co

ctural evidence of Hitler's syphilitic
ate. The fact that 'Professor'
eodore Morell, the quack doctor
o cunningly installed himself as
e Führer's personal physician, had
iginally come to the Hitler *ménage*
treat Heinrich Hoffman, Hitler's
otographer, for venereal infection
not without significance. Nor is the
ct that Helmut Spiethoff, a venereo-
gist of renown, was appointed to
tler's contingent of medicos in the
rly 1930s and the records of his
nsultations seized and impounded
the Nazi leader Wilhelm Frick when
tler became *Reichskanzler*. And both
inz Linge, his valet, and Karl
andt, surgeon to his staff, have
scribed symptoms typical of sy-
ilis in an advanced stage – maniacal
vings, palsy of the limbs, acute
pochondria, continual itching of
e skin, insomnia, and pains in the
ad and stomach.
But it is the testimony of those two
n Stefan and Daniel, given to
wyl-Davies, whose reputation as a
nereologist could not be higher,
at comes closest to proof that Hitler
ught the disease in 1910. And the
cret report shown by Himmler to
rsten can hardly be denied as
dence that its ravages continued.
e syphilis germ, *Spirochaeta pallida*,
n attack every organ in the body
d Hitler's final ravings are an almost
tain indication that the cortex of
brain had been attacked, making
neral paralysis of the insane
vitable.
The possibility of Hitler's syphilitic
te and its effect on his character
d conduct has of course been con-
ered before, though without the
porting evidence of his fellow
tims. But there has been consider-
e reluctance to accept the fact that
was infected – though for no under-
ndable reason. The social stigma
ll lingering round venereal diseases
uld scarcely have influenced the
nking of the enemies of a man
e Hitler. Better men than him
ve become infected with syphilis –

Gauguin and Schumann for example –
or – like Beethoven – inherited it, and
no one has batted an eyelid over its
effect upon their nature and work.
But even such a distinguished bio-
grapher as Alan Bullock (in his
Hitler: a Study in Tyranny) says that
'such allegations only have a place in
a study of Hitler's career if it can be
shown that [they] directly affected his
political judgments and decisions'.

Whatever the reluctance stems from
it seems to be time that it was overcome. It has now been shown, without
much room for doubt, that he was
infected. It seems equally certain that
he was not treated in time to arrest
the progress of the disease. Paul
Ehrlich's invention of 'Salvarsan 606',
which remained the standard treatment for syphilis until the arrival of
Penicillin in 1943, was announced to
the medical world at the Congress for
Internal Medicine at Wiesbaden on
19th April 1910. But it was not gener-
ally available in mass produced form
until 1912; and it is highly improbable
that Hitler, even if he'd sought treatment in the earliest stages of his
infection, could have afforded the
necessary specialist's fees for a course
of the new wonder drug. Doubtless he
had every kind of treatment after he'd
risen to power – the attachment to
the Hitler court of venereologists as
eminent as Spiethoff speaks for itself.
But by then *Spirochaeta pallida* had
latched itself irremovably on to his
system and nothing could have cured
the damage it had caused, for the
cells of the organs so attacked and
destroyed are not replaced.

Thus, with evidence rather than
'allegations' set down it is reasonable
to keep that evidence in mind while
Hitler's political and military career
is traced through its upward curve of
triumph to its ignominious end in the
bunker below the Chancellery on 30th
April 1945, when the life of the infamous Third Reich ended as in-
gloriously as that of its founder after
twelve years and four months instead
of the thousand years he had promised.

ft and *above:* Hitler the demagogue. *Below:* The end of Hitler's Reich. The
nker in Berlin is blown up

The man

Hitler left Vienna in the spring of 1913. He had by then developed gastric troubles that doubtless were the early manifestations of his untreated syphilis. He had also concentrated within himself a great deal of the anti-Jewish feeling that prevailed in the city.

It would be stretching a point to draw the conclusion that Hitler's anti-Semitism was solely the outcome of the bitterness he felt toward Hannah the Jewish whore for infecting him. That would depend on two premises: that she had been his only sexual contact – which seems improbable; and that he was aware, then, that he'd contracted the disease – which cannot be established. There can be no doubt that by the time he was certain of his infection – had been told of it, and was being treated for it, by specialists like Spiethoff and quacks like Morell – the root of his hatred could have been fed by personal revenge; he was a spiteful man. But in 1912 it is most likely that he had merely absorbed anti-Semitism as he absorbed other ideas, having nothing original of his own to offer.

Vienna at that time was rife with Anti-Semitic books and pamphle gushed from the presses – some them pornographic, most of them i sanely false in their accusations, a of them witless and insulting. The vehemence at first astonished hi 'In the Jew I still saw only a man w was of a different religion, and the fore, on grounds of human toleran I was against the idea that he shou be attacked because he had a differe faith . . . I considered that the to adopted by the anti-Semitic press Vienna was unworthy of the cultu traditions of a great people.'

But it was not long before he ov came his astonishment. 'In my ey the charge against Judaism became grave one the moment I discovered t Jewish activities in the press, in a in literature and the theatre.' He a discovered 'that nine tenths of all t smutty literature, artistic tripe a theatrical banalities, had to charged to the account' of the Je and that there was 'no form of foulne especially in cultural life, in which

An idealised portrait taken in 1933

least one Jew did not participate'.

All these remarkable discoveries, which he rants on about in the wind-blown hackneyed phrases with which *Mein Kampf* bulges, were topped by the realization 'that the Jews were the leaders of Social Democracy. In face of that revelation the scales fell from my eyes. My long inner struggle was at an end.' One can hear the scales thumping to the ground, the conflicting winds in his stomach rumbling to silence. He had at last found something to concentrate his viciousness on. But not only that. In having his mind led by way of racialism to political science he found a subject that suited both his mentality and his character. The pan-Germanic ideas that had inflected the curriculum at his Linz school now inundated his mind with swirling effect. From that vortex emerged the vision of himself as the Messianic saviour of the Aryan race – especially the German part of it. He expressed the conviction a thousand times. One of the more nauseating examples of this expression was in a pre-electoral speech in Vienna on 9th April 1938:

'I believe that it was God's will to send a boy from here into the Reich, to let him grow up, to raise him to be the leader of the nation so as to enable him to lead back his homeland into the Reich . . . to me the grace was given . . . to be able to unite my homeland with the Reich . . . may every German recognize the hour and measure its import and bow in humility before the Almighty who . . . has wrought a miracle upon us!'

That was Hitler fully developed in his megalomania. But no miracle of the Almighty had been needed to bring the embryo 'saviour' of 1912 to the megalomaniac Führer of 1938. Given a man of his instability, who was harbouring resentment against a world that failed to find any genius in him, and whose body was nurturing

Corporal Hitler (right) poses with wartime comrades

the activities of the destructive organism of syphilis, the circumstances in which such a 'saviour' could flourish had all been created by the signatories of the Treaty of Versailles.

Hitler had avoided conscription into the Austrian army in 1913 on the grounds that he refused to serve 'with filthy Czech Jews and the dregs of the Habsburg monarchy'. He left Vienna to escape service. The police, however, tenaciously pursued him with their enquiries and in January 1914 caught up with him in Munich, where he was ordered to present himself for medical examination. He was rejected, he says, because of 'poor health and general debility'. He goes on to explain that his general debility was caused by 'malnutrition consequent upon my slender earnings as an artist'. But in 1938 he ordered the Gestapo to find and destroy all records of the examination. Whatever the reason for the army's rejection of him in 1913, he was welcomed as a volunteer into the 16th Bavarian Infantry Regiment on 7th August 1914. He served as a messenger in the same regiment throughout the war, was awarded two Iron Crosses (First and Second Class) for no officially recorded reasons; and was promoted to corporal.

During a British attack on the French village of Comines on 13th October 1918 Hitler was blinded. That was the blindness mentioned in the secret report referred to by Kersten. Gas was being used by the British and it was supposed at the time to be the cause. He was sent back to hospital in Pasewalk and was there examined by an ophthalmologist, Dr Viktor Krückmann, who reported that Hitler was suffering from hysterical blindness, not from any injury caused by gas. 'It is a nervous complaint often. indicative of the tertiary stage of syphilis', he wrote. 'I advise that this man should be examined for evidence of that disease and treated accordingly. He will recover his sight.'

Which indeed he did. But of the subsequent examination by the

enereal Diseases Clinic to which he
as sent there is no record. Perhaps it
o was destroyed by the Gestapo. It
ay have been seen by the compiler
the secret document examined by
ersten, for Kersten refers to its
ention of 'symptoms associated with
philis'. But Krückmann gave it as
s opinion, in 1965, that it was deliber-
ely destroyed, just as the records of
iethoff's consultations were des-
oyed, by Frick.

At all events, Hitler was still in the
asewalk hospital when the armistice
as proclaimed, peace having been
ught by General Ludendorff of the
rman High Command and the
ancellor, Prince Max of Baden.

bove left: Hitler (back row, extreme
ght) convalescing after being
ounded, 1916. *Below left:* Ludendorff
tacks in March 1918. *Below:* By
ugust 1918, the Allies have counter-
cked; German resistance begins
crumble. German prisoners taken
ring August 1918

'In November', Hitler wrote, 'the
general tension increased. Then one
day disaster broke in upon us without warning. Sailors came in motor
lorries and called on us to rise in
revolt. A few Jew-boys were the
leaders . . . Not one of them had seen
active service at the front. Through
the medium of a hospital for venereal
diseases these three Orientals had
been sent back home. Now their red
flags were being hoisted here.'

There is no evidence whatever, other
than Hitler's spitting contempt, that
any Jews were involved, that they
were non-combatants and 'orientals',
or that they had been at a hospital
for venereal diseases. (Had he perhaps
seen them there?) The revolutionary
sailors were merely a splinter group
of the mutineers at Kiel who had
refused to take out their ships to
continue a battle that was over. But
that is just an example of Hitler's
maniacal prejudices.

In a great slab of ill-chosen words
he goes on to say that he was recover-

ing his sight and that he could scarcely believe that Germany had capitulated. 'I staggered and stumbled back to my ward and buried my aching head between the blankets and pillow . . . So all had been in vain. In vain all the sacrifices and privations, in vain the hunger and thirst for endless months, in vain those hours that we stuck to our posts though the fear of death gripped our souls . . .', and so on in an elongated saga of self-pity disguised as vengeful breast-beating. Apart from its sidelight on the character of its author that chapter of *Mein Kampf* has only one significant phrase: 'For my part I then decided that I would take up political work'.

The capitulation that so shocked Hitler – and indeed the whole German nation, which had supposed that German victory was in sight – was instigated as early as 5th October 1918. On that date a note was despatched to President Woodrow Wilson of the United States formally asking for peace negotiations. Wilson replied asking whether the German govern-

ment intended discussing peace o the terms of his addresses to Congres in which were stated the famou Fourteen Points, Four Principles an Five Particulars. The answer wa Yes. Thus it was initially agree between Germany and the Unite States that the peace negotiation should be based on a total of twenty three conditions laid down by Wilso which would have to be accepted b the Allies also. It was a shaky found ation for the discussion of a Treaty o Peace – particularly as the Allies ha had nothing but the slenderest in dication that the United States had basis of negotiation with the enemy Nor, when they heard the conditions

Below: The victors dictate peace. Lloyd George, Orlando, Clemenceau, Wilson at Versailles, 1919
Above Right: The German delegation a Versailles. Hitler called them 'the November criminals';
Below Right: Germany's air force reduced to kindling

vere they by any means inclined to accept them. Every one of the Fourteen Points was turned inside out, upside down and sideways by Clemenceau of France, Lloyd George of Britain, and Sonnino of Italy, each of whom had reasons – not all of them admirable reasons – for wishing to amend the Fourteen Points to gain specific advantages for their individual nations. But America remained adamant. The Fourteen Points must be accepted *in toto* or a separate peace would be concluded with Germany.

'This was a bombshell', says Richard I Watt in *The Kings Depart*. 'Lloyd George and Clemenceau could not possibly allow themselves to be put into the position of refusing a victorious armistice and compelling their nations to continue a now pointless war – especially when their reasons for doing so would be interreted by world opinion as a cynical rejection of such exalted principles as freedom of the seas and the abolition of secret diplomacy. [They had been] placed in a position from which there was no escape'.

It was now the turn of the Allies to capitulate. They accepted the Wilsonian principles and the armistice was concluded on 11th November. It was the opening of the door to the Versailles peace conference.

About that disastrous conference and the Treaty that was signed at it, after five months of wrangling, volumes have been written. It is necessary to say in summary only that of the conditions laid down by Wilson and accepted by the Germans no more than four were ultimately incorporated in the Treaty. The defeated enemy had signed an armistice on terms that were twisted beyond all recognition by the time the Treaty was signed. During the five months of wrangling there had been revealed attitudes of bitterness, greed and gloating revenge that, though in a way understandable, could have led only to

contention in the future – however long the clash could be postponed.

Of the plenipotentiaries of the thirty-two nations assembled at the conference Lord Keynes wrote: 'The future life of Europe was not their concern; its means of livelihood was not their anxiety. Their preoccupations, good and bad alike, related to frontiers and nationalities, to the balance of power, to imperial aggrandisements, to the future enfeeblement of a strong and dangerous enemy, to revenge, and to the shifting by the victors of their unbearable financial burdens on to the shoulders of the defeated.'

And as a further indictment of the Treaty the Prime Minister of Italy, Signor Nitti, later wrote: 'It will remain for ever a terrible precedent in modern history that, against all pledges, all precedents and traditions, the representatives of Germany were never even heard; nothing was left to them but to sign a treaty at a moment when famine and exhaustion and threat of revolution made it impossible not to sign it . . . In the old law of the Church it was laid down that everyone must have a hearing, even the devil. But the new democracy, which proposed to install the League of Nations, did not even obey the precepts which the dark Middle Ages held sacred on behalf of the accused.'

It was upon the scene created from the shambles of violated agreements, tyrannical statesmen, pistol-point force, and the dangerous humiliation of a vanquished nation, that Hitler, the man of destiny, appeared to 'take up political work'.

Hitler's greatest asset – and it amounted in its field to genius – was his psychological insight. Seeing himself as a man rejected by society, and blindly ignoring the fact that that rejection was caused by his own unendearing nature, he was readily able to identify himself with the masses of a nation that, merely seeking an honourable peace, had been kicked and ground into the dust by the

The Nazi leader in Bavarian *Lederhosen*

ersailles Treaty. Humiliation is the most dangerous of all punishments to mete out to a nation not abject in character; and a man who can play on the emotions of a people forced to grovel cannot fail to find a hearing. Certainly not in the circumstances afflicting post-war Germany.

But it was by no means an immediate hearing. Even an inherent genius has to be guided along a profitable path. So far as Hitler was concerned the path lay through the taverns of Munich where, in 1919, he fortuitously found himself among men who later were to become famous as his teachers and associates – Dietrich Eckart, Ernst Röhm, Alfred Rosenberg, Rudolf Hess, Anton Drexler, Karl Harer, and Gottfried Feder. Those men – a poet, a soldier, an architect, a politician disguised as a military adviser, a locksmith, a journalist, and a slightly dotty scientist-cum-economist – were all floundering in a treacly mess of misbegotten revolutionary notions for the rescue of Germany from the disastrous state of affairs wrought by the war and the Treaty of Peace.

It was Eckart who fidgeted endlessly over the formation of a 'German Citizen Party' to counteract the influence of Bolsheviks and Jews, and who described the character of the man who must lead it:

'We must have a fellow at the top who won't wince at the rattle of a machine-gun. The mob must be given a damned good fright. An officer won't do; the people don't respect them any more. Best of all would be a workman in a soldier's coat and with his tongue in his cheek. He needn't be very brainy; politics is the most imbecile business in the world and every market-woman in Munich knows as much as those fellows in Weimar. I'd rather have a stupid, vain jackanapes who can give the Reds a juicy

We must have a fellow at the top who won't wince at the rattle of a machine-gun'

answer and not run away whenever a chair-leg is aimed at him, than a dozen learned professors who sit trembling on the wet trousers-seat of facts. Also he must be a bachelor. Then we shall get the women!'

But it was Anton Drexler who actually founded the party that Hitler was to lead, the German Workers' Party, a lacklustre, static group with forty members and a total capital of 7.50 marks. And it was while attending one of its feeble political meetings on 12th September 1919 that he spoke with such vehemence that Drexler persuaded him to join the committee of six. He had been sent to the meeting as a minor spy in the service of the Munich army command, which was prodding to detect subversive political activities. But what he actually detected was the chance of a lifetime. Here was an aimless, poorly conducted organization full of nonentities; and although he was himself a nonentity he had ideas far above that station and immediately saw the possibility of imposing them on a floundering body that lacked leadership, energy and members.

Almost at once he assumed command; implicitly if not by title; and three months later he was appointed Propaganda Officer. (Hitler's brilliance as publicist has been fully explored in *The Nuremberg Rallies*, Campaign Book 8 in this series.) He brought about the amalgamation with several other minor movements whose aims, vaguely, were the practical implementation of a policy of anti-Semitism and anti-Communism, and the non-fulfilment of the oppressive conditions of the Versailles Treaty. And he blew up the title into the grandiose *Nationalsozialistische Deutsche Arbeiterpartei*, (National Socialist German Workers' Party), from the first word of which the abbreviation Nazi was manufactured. The fortunes of the Nazi Party, and subsequently of the Third Reich, over the next twenty-five years, are the fortunes of Adolf Hitler.

The demagogue

Like Hitler, the Party was diseased. It was the disease of neurotic vainglory. Those with an interest in the study of theories of racialism can examine the symptoms exhibited by such mighty bores as Thomas Wolfe, Houston Stewart Chamberlain, the Comte de Gobineau and Chamberlain's father-in-law Richard Wagner. They all lead back to the myths of heroic Aryan Siegfrieds, hideous racially inferior Alberichs, and Valhallas fit for triumphant German gods to live in. People dissatisfied with reality create legends; and the wretched realities of the Versailles Treaty and the Weimar Republic impelled every kind of sick grievance needing only the solace of a tale-telling healer to ease the malaise. Houston Stewart Chamberlain, after having his boots unctuously glossed with Hitler's lick-spittle admiration, declared:

'The fact that at the hour of her deepest need Germany has given birth to a Hitler proves her vitality.'

What it in fact proved was the Party's inability to provide any alternative to the vindictive evils into which Germany had been ground by Versailles other than the falsely glamorous Valhalla now revealed in prestigious glimpses by the marketing methods of their Pied Piper saviour.

In the same way in which Hitler had assumed command of the nonentities of the German Workers' Party in 1919, he had by 1923 gathered in his wake some 55,000 unorganized Germans – most of them from the south – who characteristically malleable, were easily shaped to the aggressive Nazi pattern. His first attempt at overt aggression was to surround himself with a body of witless roughnecks and burst into a Munich hall where a political meeting was being staged by a rival group. He fired pistol shots at the ceiling, shrieked out that the Bavarian government was now deposed, and that he himself was the leader of the new Reich. Understandably, this melodramatic coup failed (though only just), and to save face he staged a demonstration march next day, 9th November 1923. That march, which he led side by side with Ludendorff, encountered thin police resistance and shots were fired from both sides. Hitler bolted, leaving the bodies of sixteen dead Nazis in the Odeonplatz. (They were later to be made the most famous martyrs of the Nazi cause, and Hitler was to justify his unseemly disappearance from the fray by explaining that he had 'carried a helpless child out of the firing line'. There was no child; and if there had been, Hitler could not have carried it because before bolting he had fallen heavily and dislocated his right shoulder and broken his left arm.)

The direct result of the 9th Novem

Hitler in characteristic stance, November 1933, after coming to power. Röhm and Himmler to right

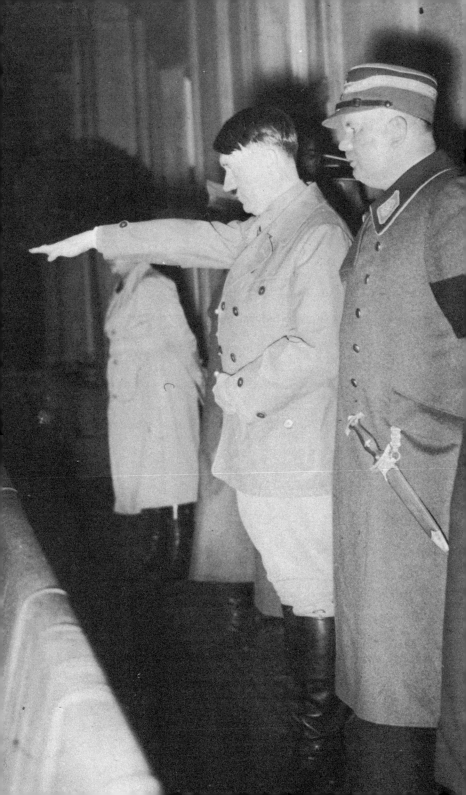

Houston Stewart Chamberlain

Richard Wagner

ber *putsch* was that Hitler was arrested for treason, tried and given a mandatory sentence of five years' imprisonment, and confined in the greatest comfort in Landsberg fortress. He was allowed special food, visitors, a comfortable room, flowers, a private secretary, and unlimited exercise in the grounds; and was released after eight months, his defence speech to the Munich People's Court having been so full of lofty patriotic guff that their verdict of 'guilty' had been found only after assurances from the president that the accused would be granted an early pardon.

During his imprisonment he wrote – if it can be called writing – the tedious *Mein Kampf*. The Party had been proscribed, but its surreptitious revival had been the matter of much quarrelling among some of Hitler's leading henchmen – Strasser, Streicher, Röhm, Rosenberg, Ludendorff, Feder and Frick – who fought over the political corpse like hyenas. Hitler loftily dissociated himself from their disagreements on aims and leadership and engaged in the literary life, dictating much of *Mein Kampf* to Rudolf Hess, who acted as his secretary. It was no wish of his to have the Party come to life again under someone else's leadership. He waited till he was released on parole then persuaded the Bavarian Minister

of Justice to allow the re-formatic of the Party and the re-publication its newspaper the *Volkischer Be bachter*. His persuasion was based an admission of all his past mistak and a declaration that the Nazis h only the single object of fightin Marxism and Judaism. There was glutinous reconciliation between hi and some of the bickering leaders, a the Party was once again a for in the field.

For a long time, though, it was extremely ineffective force. Thou he had acceded to Hitler's abject ple the Minister of Justice had not be so stupid as to allow him to ma speeches. That was very wise. It w only the mesmeric personality pr jected through the hysterical speech that brought the Party its adheren But wisdom could not be sustaine The ban on Hitler's speeches was lift in May 1927 and the quasi-religio cult of the saviour spread amo thousands more who listened to h with an hysteria matching his ow an hysteria which was, as Hitl himself put it, not involuntary but tactic based on the precise calculati of all human weaknesses, the resu of which must lead almost matl matically to success'.

Which of course it did. He was rapist using a phallus of wor Eckhart had been fortuitously rig when he had drawn the pattern for t

ader: 'He must be a bachelor. Then
e shall get the women!' The masses
ere indeed to him 'women'. Coarse
kes were made about his own state-
ent that after a big speech he was
oaking wet'; but it was true that he
perienced orgiastic delirium – 'a
bstitute', as Joachim Fest has put
, 'for the emotional experience that
d remained closed to him in all his
onstrous egofixation'. Possibly, too,
one concedes that he was a rapist,
so an act of revenge against the
philitic Hannah. He had written
verishly in *Mein Kampf* on syphilis
d Jewish genetics, and that too may
ve been subconscious – or even deli-
rate – vengeance on a person rather
an a race.

As for more normal sexual relation-
ips, there has been much specu-
tion about Hitler's explorations in
at direction, but very few known
cts to support it. In his youth there
as the unattainable Stefanie and the
l-too-easily attainable Hannah; in
iddle age his supposed mistress Eva
raun, whom he married as a prelude
the suicide pact that ended their
ves. And during the days of the rise of
e Party in the late 1920s he lived
ith his niece, Geli Raubal, daughter
his step-sister Angela. Geli shot
rself in Hitler's flat in Munich in
31 and for a time he appeared to be
consolable; but that proves nothing
cept an emotional fixation on a girl
venty years younger than him-
lf whom he had characteristically
rannized into a state of neurotic
bjection. Because of its deterio-
tive effect on his mind and body, the
ief encounter with Hannah is enor-
ously important; but all other
delights on Hitler's sexual en-
avours can be switched to the realm
conjecture.

In contrast, everything about the
esmeric influence and growth of the
rty under Hitler's leadership is
pported by facts. There were minor
sagreements within the organi-
tion – mainly centred in the raffish
orm Troopers who had been re-
cruited from the ex-service men who
formed the tiny army permitted by
the Versailles Treaty and who displayed more military than political
enthusiasm, which at the time didn't
suit Hitler's book at all. (Hitler allowed them to choke themselves with
their own war-cries and by 1929 had
set up his own *corps d'élite* under
the sinister leadership of Heinrich
Himmler. The SS – *Schutz Staffeln* or
blackshirted bodyguard – had political
enthusiasm enough and were sworn to
absolute obedience; and it was eventually through them that Hitler
dominated Party, nation and armed
forces.) In spite of such internal
discord, however, the Party increased
its grip on the country. Having fallen
to 17,000 in 1926, the restoration in 1927
of Hitler's right to make public
speeches quickly brought the membership to 60,000 in 1928; and one may
certainly infer at least twice that
number who were supporters if not
actual members of the Party.

But it was with the American
financial crisis of 1929, and the suc-
ceeding economic depression in the
West, that Hitler and the Nazi Party
rose to victory. Under the Weimar
Republic, which Hitler referred to
variously as the 'republic of betrayal',
'the November criminals' and 'the
Jew-ridden traitors', American money
had poured into Germany. The mark
had been stabilized; Allied forces
withdrawn from the Rhineland, and
industrial production increased to an
extent that had reduced unemploy-
ment to little more than half a
million. Against such prosperity the
Nazis had little hope of making much
headway with their doom-laden pro-
phecies of forthcoming financial disaster. They polled fewer than a million
votes at the 1928 elections and were
represented by only twelve seats in
the Reichstag. But with the Wall
Street crash of 1929 disaster came.
Germany's inability to repay either
the iniquitous reparations demanded
by the Versailles Treaty or the interest on the short-term loans that

Above: Hitler, Julius Streicher, and other leaders at a German Day rally, September, 1923. *Below:* The treason trial following the unsuccessful Munich putsch of November 1923, Ludendorff arrives at the court

Above: With party comrades during his imprisonment at Landsberg (Hess second from right). *Below:* In 1927, after having spoken in Berlin for the first time

Eva Braun with Hitler

Geli Raubal, Hitler's niece and greatest love

eft: Now Reich Chancellor, Hitler
greets the ageing President
Hindenburg, 1933 *Above:* Rapturous
crowds greet their Führer

ad so readily been made by an
America dizzy with her own power,
insured an immediate economic
plunge. She was like a man who has
been leapfrogging cheques into and
out of his bank account and is suddenly let down by the non-arrival of the
credit intended to cover the post-
dated debit made the day before
yesterday and due to be presented
today. By 1932 there were five million
unemployed. The disease of hopelessness spread throughout the country.
Food, warmth and shelter were pulled
out of the people's grasp with terrible
frequency. Even if a breadwinner was
working he was unlikely to be working
in full time. Savings vanished in a
wave of profiteering and a desperate
effort to pay the mortgages on farms
and houses. And, as Alan Bullock says
in *Hitler: a Study in Tyranny:*

'Like men and women in a town
stricken by an earthquake, millions of
Germans saw the apparently solid
framework of their existence cracking
and crumbling. In such circumstances

men are no longer amenable to the
arguments of reason. In such circumstances men entertain fantastic fears,
extravagant hatreds and extravagant
hopes. In such circumstances the
extravagant demagogy of Hitler began
to attract a mass following as it had
never done before.'

That mass following, coupled with
the inability of his opponents to
compete with his propaganda
methods, and reinforced by his own
cunning intrigues to subvert – by
threat, bribery, murder or any other
method that served the purpose – the
efforts of those Party members who
were themselves jostling for power,
brought Hitler to the Chancellorship
of the German Reich in January 1933.
On the death of President von Hindenberg nineteen months later he announced – with the coerced agreement
of those who had in some ways
attempted to restrain his rise to power
– that the offices of President and
Chancellor were united and that he
himself was now Supreme ruler of the
State and Commander-in-Chief of all
the armed forces.

His first command to his army was
to swear an oath of allegiance and
obedience to him personally – not to

Below: Hitler's first cabinet. Göring and Papen in front row. *Above:* 13th June 1934, Hitler warns the Reichstag that 'the Wehrmacht is the only instrument of war.' *Right:* On 30th June, Ernst Röhm (right) and many of his SA lieutenants are summarily executed

the Constitution or the country:

'I swear by God this holy oath: I will render unconditional obedience to the Führer of the German Reich and People, Adolf Hitler, the Supreme Commander of the Armed Forces, and will be ready, as a brave soldier, to give my life at any time for my Führer.'

Thus, by August 1934, Adolf Hitler had manoeuvred himself into a position of absolute power. The corruptive effects of that power were soon to become apparent.

Hitler's personal ruthlessness toward rivals or dissentients had been shockingly manifested in a purge five weeks earlier. On 30th June he ordered the execution of Ernst Röhm and other leaders of the Storm Troopers who had attempted a revolt. There were massacres all over Germany. The ex-Chancellor, General von Schleicher, and prominent army officers, civil servants and Roman Catholics were murdered. The assassins were the black-shirted SS who, together with the Gestapo, were from now on t become the chief executants of Hitler' machinations.

Politically and socially there wer less murderous but equally effectiv forms of ruthlessness. The entir parliamentary system of the Weima republic was dissolved. All politica parties except the Nazis were banne To found any kind of non-Naz political organization became pun shable by heavy terms of imprison ment. Freedom of cultural expressio in art and literature was no mor Civil rights and equality of citizenshi were suppressed and the 'leader' sys tem introduced – an all-powerfu Führer at the top and innumerabl lesser Führers step-dancing on th heads of their inferiors in rank righ down to the ordinary citizen for who there could be no leadership until had found someone to lead. Inst tutions such as education, Church an press were revolutionized. Only th Nazi version of Germany's history wa

Indem ich mich des Juden erwehre kämpfe ich für das Werk des Herrn

ti-Semitic propaganda. *Left:* 'By
sisting the Jews I fight for the Lord'
oclaims a banner. *Above:* Der Stürmer
splayed on a Berlin notice-board

ld, only the anti-Jewish religion of
opaganda was tolerated, the press
as the mouthpiece of Nazidom and no
her voice was to be heard.

For four years Hitler built up the
azi state into a diplomatic and mili-
ry machine that violated most of
e principal clauses of the Versailles
reaty. He founded the Luftwaffe,
troduced military conscription,
cupied the demilitarized Rhineland
ith his troops; he withdrew from the
orld disarmament conference, aban-
ned Germany's membership of the
eague of Nations, concluded a pres-
gious concordat with the Vatican
d a non-aggression pact with Poland
both of which were meant to allow
me for his designs to mature, not to
ve Italy or Poland any peaceful
dvantages.

Those four years from 1933 to 1937
saw the economic recovery of the
German nation and the swelling of her
armed forces to an immense aggressive power that baffled and frustrated
the member countries of the League
of Nations (from which Japan and
Italy, as well as Germany, had resigned). Hitler's psychological insight
had proved to be brilliant. With a
series of bold strokes of diplomacy
he had foxed the statesmen who
played the diplomatic game by conventional rules. By the time they had
shaken off their gentlemanly attitude
and realized that they were dealing
with a brilliant psychopath the
strands of the Führer's plans for
German domination had become in-
extricably knotted round the unwary
victims. By the spring of 1938 Hitler
was strong enough to bring off a
bloodless invasion of Austria and
annex it into the German Reich.
Henceforward the land of his own
birth ceased to exist as a name.

But his maniacal lust for *lebensraum*
and power were by no means so

45

German rearmament. *Above:* Hitler reviews new Wehrmacht units. *Below:*
Infantry and PzKpfw III tanks give a battle demonstration. Nuremberg 1938

German conquest. *Above:* The Anschluss of Austria, March 1938. *Below:* Hitler rides in triumph through Carlsbad, Czechoslovakia, October 1938

The Nazi-Soviet Non-Aggression Pact of 1939. Hitler and Molotov in conference

easily sated. Britain and France having pusillanimously betrayed Czechoslovakia into withdrawing her defensive forces from the Sudetenland to give themselves time to prepare for a war whose inevitability they had ensured, Hitler occupied that territory without having to strike a blow, in the autumn of 1938. Six months later he spread his talons into Bohemia, Moravia and Memel. The Free State of Danzig was proclaimed part of the German Reich on 1st September 1939, and Poland was invaded without warning or provocation at dawn on the same day, thus forcing Britain and France to declare war to back their treaty obligations to Poland.

A week before the holocaust of war was loosed upon Europe Hitler had brought off his crowning stroke of diplomacy: a non-aggression and trade pact with Russia 'guaranteeing' peace between the two countries for a minimum of ten years. Since he had been preaching against the wickedness of Communism since 1919 the pact was a masterstroke. The theoretical cost of it was considerable: nothing less than the division of the ill-fated Poland into two equal parts – the easternmost of which would be Russia's prize. But the worthlessness of the Pact can be measured by Hitler's revelation of his eventual aim, made at a conference with his military chiefs on 22nd August: 'My pact is only meant to stall for time, gentlemen. We will crush the Soviet Union'. Time indeed was of the essence for his schemes. For Germany to fight, even in her present state of immense military power, on both Western and Eastern fronts simultaneously would have been as fatal in 1939 as it had proved to be in the First World War. The West must be crushed first. And immediately he received the Allies' declaration of war on 3rd September 1939 Hitler set about his gigantic task.

The General

With his attack upon Poland Hitler had not only precipitated the war but could claim that no state of war had existed until the Allies declared it. Reduced to the status of a children's backyard fight, it was '*I* didn't start it, *he* did'. The invasion of Poland was merely, by Hitlerian standards, a logical and justifiable extension of his claim to the Free State of Danzig and, earlier, to Austria, the Sudetenland, Bohemia, Moravia and Memel. These, as he had argued interminably, were part of the German Reich, from which they had been chipped away in the rapacious carve-up after the First World War. He could also point to the fact that not a drop of blood had been shed in his 'liberation' of their people from the oppressive yoke of Versailles. Had the Poles shown a similar sensible willingness to be embraced by the Reich there would have been no need for coercion.

The speciousness of such argument would of course have been apparent to any impartial tribunal investigating the immediate causes of the war. But there was no such tribunal and no such argument.

Poland was virtually conquer within a matter of hours. Mastery the air was easily attained by an al out offensive beginning at dawn 1st September. Waves of bombe simply flew over Polish aerodrom and bombed the planes on the groun Those that got into the air were sh down by the bombers' fighter escort which then descended to roof-top lev and machine-gunned the planes ar personnel that had survived tl bombing. With no defence again further air attacks the Poles the were completely vulnerable so far bridges, marshalling yards, produ tion centres, military installatio and mobile columns were concerne The Polish defence forces numbere nearly two million; but the Germa air attack had ensured that they cou not be effectively mobilized, since a communications were thrown in utter confusion.

No aspect of the Polish campaig should have surprised anybody, lea

The corporal and his generals. Hitler with Blomberg and Fritsch before thei dismissal

of all the Poles. It was entirely consistent with Hitler's methods. (The Russians, despite being bonded with Germany by the non-aggression pact, were, in less than two years' time, to experience precisely the same way of opening the attack upon them by the bombing of their aerodromes; and they were equally unprepared.) But the Polish forces were being assembled to defend a leisurely attack by the traditional methods of 1914. Their Commander-in-Chief, Marshal Smigly-Rydz, seems first to have been disarmed – in the non-military sense – by Hitler's assurance given via Göring in 1937 that Germany had no territorial interest in Poland, and secondly, when attack by Germany was clearly imminent, to have supposed that the attack would go by the rules of the 1914 book.

It may seem somewhat feeble to point through the glass of hindsight to Hitler's obvious contempt for the rules of any outmoded book that did

Spearhead of the blitzkrieg. *Above:* **Me-109E fighters and Me-110 fighter bombers over Poland.** *Right:* **Stukas approach their target**

not, so to speak, suit his own boo But clearly it was not obvious, or el was incredible, at the time. Not on the Polish but the military theoris of Britain and France too suffer from the hangover of thinking terms of cavalry charges and oth outmoded ploys; and in the early stag of the war were continually dum founded by Hitler's ruthless but pe fectly logical planning and executio

That skill has since come to marvelled at as Hitler's 'intuitio There has been a tendency to suppo that he had some almost supernatur power that enabled him to anticipa the military moves of his opponents or, rather, in the early stages of t war, the lack of any ability on the pa of his mightiest opponents, t French, to make any moves at a except of the most pusillanimous kind. But Hitler had no supernatural powers. He was not in league with any necromancers. His 'intuition' was no more than the psychological insight that had enabled him to identify himself with the nation humiliatingly vanquished by Versailles. It was simply a sound understanding of human nature in general and of his opponents' characters in particular. (It was not, in the particular sense, an unfailing understanding, as was to be proved by his ignorance of the American character; but its occasional failures proved that there was nothing supernatural about it.) Just as he knew, and had unequivocally stated in *Mein Kampf*, that the endless reiteration of a demonstrable lie turns it effectively into a demonstrable truth, so he knew that he had virtually nothing to fear from the French in 1939.

He had correctly deduced that after the First World War the French would be obsessed with defence, with security within their own boundaries. The two successive post-war Commanders-in-Chief, Pétain and Weygand, had made it very clear. The people had seen the futile massacre of French youth in the bloody offensive designed by General Nivelle in 1917; they were in no heart to tolerate any more Generals of like mind. Nor had they any interest in extending their frontiers. They would spend years licking their terrible wounds and millions of francs barricading themselves in. The French Third Republic was in danger of collapse and the dignity of French civilization had been cracked by a profitless victory in 1918. Only mighty bastions behind which they could brood and build up a huge army of defending Frenchmen would satisfy the nation.

In all this Hitler was correct – and indeed it needed little in the way of psychological understanding to perceive the obvious. The impregnable fortifications to be built in the name

Germany, Aug.1939

Apr 1940 Dates of German Occupation
          or Invasion

0 Miles 100   200   300   400
0 Kilometres 200   400   600

Kristiansand
Tro...
And...
NORW...
Bergen   Apr.19
              0
Stavanger

NORTH SEA

DENM...
Apr 1
...

EIRE
Dublin

GREAT
BRITAIN
London   Amsterdam
                NETH.
                May 1940

Mar.1936
RHINELAND
Cologne   Weimar
Calais BELG.
Dieppe Brussels
Cherbourg   Wiesbaden
        Le Havre LUX.   Frankfurt
Brest   Caen   Soissons SIEGFRIED
        NORMANDY Compeigne LINE
BRITTANY   Paris   Karlsruhe
                 Seine   Meuse
                         Nure...
                 MAGINOT
                 LINE   Munic...
        Nantes   Landsberg
                         Berchtes...
FRANCE   A...
        May 1940 Berne
                  SWITZ.

ATLANTIC

OCEAN   Milan

                         I...

                 Marseilles

Lisbon   Madrid   Corsica

PORTUGAL SPAIN

                         Sardinia

Gibraltar

MEDITERRANEAN SEA

ALGERIA

Hitler's European Empire

Above: Smigly-Rydz, the Polish commander *Left:* Panzer troops rest on their advance into Poland

of the War Minister, André Maginot, were begun in 1930.

Superficially, the Maginot Line made up in impregnability for what it lacked in sense. (It left undefended the frontier to Belgium, through whose militarily ideal terrain the Germans had since time immemorial always attacked France.) But impregnability in this case was nothing but a comforting illusion, an almost literal sticking of heads into the sand – for the elaborate fortifications were built deep into the ground. They were burrows fitted out with stores and ammunition, with comforts and communications to withstand any siege. The mighty guns of the Line faced Germany and were protected by impenetrable steel and concrete. The 'tombstone of France' – as Major-General J F C Fuller has called it – had cost some £40,000,000, which is a lot of money for a soporific; but that is what it turned out to be. The French did not want to fight; their enormous army – there were at least twenty-six Divisions in the Maginot Line alone – was

eft: Weygand (second from right) with *riand, Lloyd George, and Foch. **Above:** *étain*

Above: André Maginot, French *Minister of War in the early thirties. Left:* A section of the Maginot line

riddled with treachery from top to bottom and wanted nothing more active (as Fuller put it) than to 'sit in the Maginot Line, snip up *La Vie Parisienne*, decorate their dugouts with very unsatisfying young ladies, and cry to go home'.

By the time the Maginot Line was finished in 1935 Hitler was in complete power as Führer, Chancellor, President, absolute despot and Pied Piper of the German nation. This unlovable man had succeeded, like a carrier of typhoid, in spreading the disease of vainglory among the Party, and with the help of skilful publicists like Göbbels and monstrous jamborees like the Nuremberg Rallies, would spread it throughout the nation – aided by the national susceptibility to wallow in the myth of the Master Race. In doing that he had forged a mighty sword. It was the sword of confidence. Mesmerised by their Führer's ceaseless reiteration of the theme and the endless chain of variations upon it the Germans danced to the tune of ecstatic triumph.

The confidence of France being reposed in nothing but the impregnability of the Maginot Line, it is not surprising to hear Hitler saying to the British journalist G Ward Price at Berchtesgaden in 1938, 'I have studied the Maginot Line and learned much from it'. The much he had learned from it came from very little study. The Line ended where the Belgian frontier began; there was no need to study it any more. As for the vast numbers of French soldiers locked defensively in it, 'It is an axiom of the art of war that the side which stays within its fortifications is beaten'. The tag was Napoleon's but the truth of it was as old as war. Only a minuscule number of French militarists unburied their heads from the Maginot sands long enough to shout words of warning. One was Colonel de Gaulle, another was General Guillaumat:'It is dangerous to let the false and demoralizing notion spread that once we have fortifications the inviola-

The SS became the Nazi élite. *Above:* Hitler's personal SS bodyguard. *Below* and *right:* Himmler grew to be one of the most powerful men in the Nazi hierarchy

lity of our country is assured, and
.at they are a substitute for the rude
bour of preparation of wills, hearts
d minds'. No-one heeded the shouts.
1e French people were asleep, drug-
d by their Maginot potion. They
ere morally rotten, physically flabby,
d apparently mentally deficient.
It is the business of a general, as the
storian Polybius pointed out two
ousand years ago, to create a
arlike spirit, 'for of all the forces in
ur that is the most influential'. It is
so the business of the general to
rn to his own advantage those
eapons aligned against him. For the
st, Hitler had built up the morale of
e German people to a state that was
uivalent to numerical superiority in
en and weapons; for the second, *inter
ia* he had intrigued to infiltrate the
ostile ideology of Communism into
ance, where it had completed the
moralization of the people with its
int. Thus, up to 3rd Spetember 1939,
had created favourable conditions.
it with the invasion of Poland and
e inevitable consequent declaration
war by France and Britain he had
rced an issue that would put his
neralship to a greater test.

It was one of Hitler's characteristics
at he could not delegate. It was a
tural corollary of his despotism. He
inted to make all the decisions and
ke all the responsibility; and if he
d been able to assume god-like
ntrol of everything from the grand
rategy to the design of his troops'
ttons he would have been a god-like
neral. Intervening between him and
at state, however, were the generals
his High Command, who were
erely human, with no god-like
pirations, and who were much abler
ministrators than their Führer,
ho hated systematic work as much
he hated delegation of power.

Normal military practice is to ap-
oint commanders for their expertise
in various aspects of strategic affairs,
to consult them, and to co-ordinate
their advice. An overall plan of
campaign is then evolved and the
commanders directed to carry it out
in its various stages.

Hitler worked the other way round.
His hatred of delegation was based on
distrust. Like all megalomaniacs he
was fearful of rivalry, of any other
hand than his own on the reins of
power. When in Landsberg fortress he
had cunningly detached himself from
all attempts by his henchmen to
revive the proscribed Nazi party
because he could not himself have led
it while still serving a prison sentence.
After his release, though, he set about
the restoration of the Party, and his
own leadership of it, very swiftly. And
his achievement of absolute political
power during the first half of the
nineteen-thirties was crowned by
his own decree, which stated un-
quivocally: 'From henceforth I exercise personally the immediate command over the whole armed forces'.

Since even Hitler could see the
impracticability of extending his command like a web throughout all the
ramifications of organization, he made
a gesture to military orthodoxy by
establishing a High Command. It was,
however, a body controlled by Hitler's
lackey favourites rather than a consultative and advisory committee rich
with influence. It served as a computer
to work out the details of Hitler's
grand designs. It also reported to him
what was practical and what not, and
in that sense may perhaps be said to
have been advisory. But its master's
mind was already made up on every
point. When decision coincided with
advice the High Command appeared to
be working in the orthodox way; when
its recommendations were torn to
shreds in turbulent scenes at what
with Hitler passed for 'conferences',
and he spat out his refusal to consider any question of emendation
– then the Führer appeared to be
ironwilled and brilliantly perceptive
in a setup that surrounded him

hen giving speeches or holding
nferences, Hitler often worked
mself up into a state of frenzy

with blockheads.

Naturally the army chiefs were often aroused to bitter resentment by such treatment. They were, after all, experienced strategists who could present an appreciation of any military situation. To be contemptuously treated because their appreciations took no account of the political manoeuvres of statesmen was humiliating. And humiliation, as had been proved by the entire course of post-Versailles German history, is extremely dangerous. It resulted in brooding conspiracies that were eventually suppressed only by the infiltration of Himmler's secret police into the armed forces. Some were never entirely suppressed in spite of the SS chief's serpentine activities. A plot to kidnap and overthrow Hitler was – ironically – frustrated only by Chamberlain's trembling supplications at Munich in 1938. The attempted murder in the bomb plot of 20th July 1944 failed only in the degree of its effectiveness. And there were at least five other attempts on his life.

All dictators are subject to the envious attempts of rival megalomaniacs to usurp their power; but those of Hitler's generals who plotted against him were more concerned to abort the disasters they saw germinate in his decisions. They insistently advised him against attacking Czechoslovakia in 1938. 'He was like a man demented', says Brauchitsch, Commander-in-Chief of the army, of an occasion when the High Command was standing firm. 'He was sweating and shrieking, there was froth on his lips, his speech was incoherent for many minutes. Only after a frightening storm did we make out that it was "his unalterable will to smash Czechoslovakia by military action in the near future".'

The frustrating thing for the High Command was that Hitler was proved right time and time again. It was only because he had weakened the

ft: **The newly re-armed Wehrmacht**
ters the Rhineland. *Above:* **The SA,**
first the Army's main threat

etical brilliance by his distrust that
eir function as a consultative and
ministrative body failed him when
st needed in the later vital cam-
igns of the war. But none of them
ıld deny that, rightly or wrongly,
e carried on his own back' (as Alan
ark says in *Barbarossa*) 'the res-
nsibility for every decision of
portance and formulated in his own
nd the development of his strategic
ıbition in its entirety'.

His contempt for the High Command
s often voiced in such inaccurate
neralisations as: 'No general will
er pronounce himself ready to
tack; and no commander will ever
ht a defensive battle without look-
g over his shoulder to a "shorter
e".' He was himself an inspired
nateur of military strategy. He
ew all the theories according to
Clausewitz, the classic battles of
Darius and Alexander, the manoeuvres
of Hannibal at Cannae and Frederick
the Great at Leuthen; and though he
very rarely visited the front line
throughout the war he had a sound
understanding of the fighting soldier
and his needs. He had, after all, been
one himself; and presumably his Iron
Cross had been awarded for some act
of courage, though the citation was
never publicized. (Perhaps it was
suppressed as unworthy by the bur-
rowing Gestapo men who in 1938 had
destroyed the records of his 1914
medical examination and the records
of the Venereal Diseases Clinic to
which he was sent in 1918.) Anyway,
one may look charitably upon his
somewhat speedy departure from the
scene of action on 9th November 1923
and say that courage is a virtue only
insofar as it is directed by prudence.

The ways in which he expressed his
contempt for the High Command are
less revealing than the reasons for it.

One must include among possible reasons the adolescent hatred he had felt for the officer class exemplified by the corseted, scented socialites who had, he believed, stolen Stefanie's affections. Also, there was plenty of evidence that in the First World War the German General Staff had hastened America's entry into the war by introducing unrestricted submarine attacks; had destroyed hopes of peace with Russia by demanding that a Kingdom of Poland should be established and by returning Lenin and his émigré colleagues from Geneva to Russia in 1917; and had mis-managed the Verdun battle of 1916 and thus prolonged the war. Those were errors of political and military strategy that justified censoriousness. But there was a deeper-rooted cause of his contempt: the reactionary spirit that, he said, riddled the upper echelons of the army as a result of 'Habsburg effeteness, Jewish cunning, and the Masonic disease of favouritism in high places'.

Whether his contempt was at bottom much more than a manifestation of his megalomania can be left for t moment. On the Allies' declaration war on 3rd September 1939 Hit could well afford to laugh in Generals' faces. They had no record brilliance to justify themselves. Su appreciations as they had put befo him during the founding of th Führer's 'Thousand-year Reich' h been discarded with despotic fury coldly ignored. From the time wh they had advised against the reoc pation of the Rhineland as the fi extension of Reich tentacles, to th recent insistent warnings agai attacking Czechoslovakia they h been wrong. And even as open war w declared by Britain and France th had the baffling satisfaction of see Poland fall to their armies w scarcely more than a trifling effo The High Command faced their S reme Commander sheepishly, fear of his intuitions. Where next wo they lead?

Below: The British declare war. Woul they help Poland? *Right:* The Führer. A flattering portrait by Hoffmann

The General in action

Though the fate of Poland was to all intents and purposes sealed within a few hours of the *coup* of 1st September, acknowledged defeat was delayed until the 27th, ten days after the government had interned itself in Rumania. On that day Warsaw surrendered after devastating air and artillery attacks. Like cats glutted with cream the two 'victorious' nations claimed that there was no longer anything to fight for:

'After the definite settlement of the problems arising from the collapse of the Polish state it will serve the true interest of all peoples to put an end to the state of war existing between Germany on the one hand and England and France on the other.'

Thus Ribbentrop and Molotov as the joint mouthpiece of Hitler. It was a worthless peace offer, no more than a façade of good intentions. Hitler had already secretly declared to the High Command his determination to crush Russia, as we have seen. Peace in the West would have suited that purpose, certainly, and to sue for it was a politically sound move since it ga the impression that his territori demands truly were ended and that was aggrieved rather than aggressiv ('Hitler's Peace offer – No War Air Against Britain and France – Redu tion of Armaments – Peace Co ference' – the headlines shrieked fro the *Völkischer Beobachter;* and wh Chamberlain and Daladier reject the hollow offer even bigger ty announced 'Britain Chooses War But all such overtures were no mo than attempts at self-vindicatic Now that they had been sniffily turn down Hitler's larger designs could pursued. 'I am determined to a aggressively and without much dela he said on 9th October in Directi No. 6. Russia, soothed with a peac and-trade pact and half of Poland as material prize, could wait whi Western Europe was dealt with.

Strategically, Britain and Fran had played into Hitler's hands. Mu of the enormous French army w

Hitler with Admiral Raeder

cringing in the Maginot Line; the British Expeditionary Force under Lord Gort tardily arrived in France during the autumn and winter. The two Allies had manoeuvred themselves into the position of being bound by treaty to aid Poland. Now, with Poland overcome in a débacle they sat glumly wondering what to do next. With more than a hundred divisions of French soldiers spread across France and Hitler's effective strength concentrated in Poland throughout September and well into October, the Allies sat and paused to consider their course of action, if any.

Hitler did not wonder what to do next. Conveniently for him, part of the BEF straddled the River Lys along the Franco-Belgian frontier. An excuse was thus ready made to overrun France to 'prevent the clear intention of the British and French forces to invade the Low Countries' – a typically Hitlerian gambit.

His generals, well aware of their military weakness everywhere except in Poland, and again basing their strategy on what Hitler described as 'outmoded and weak notions', saw no sense in extending a war that could well be triumphantly concluded by compromise if the Franco-British defensive enemy were not forced into action. They produced excuse after excuse for inaction: the coming winter, the impregnability of the Maginot Line, doubts whether the forces in Poland could be re-equipped and transferred to the West, the huge losses that would have to be faced ... Their excuses were, to be sure, based largely on conventional military thought; but there was too an underlying distrust of their Führer's leadership. His ruthlessness had too often been expressed in extreme forms of violence toward those who opposed him – as in the purge of June 1934. The distrust led to conspiratorial designs on his life. One of them appeared to be within a streak of success when a

Poland. *Above left:* Hitler watches troops cross the frontier, 1st September 1939.
Above and *below:* Victory parade through Warsaw

Above: General Brauchitsch.
Right: The scuttled Graf Spee on fire off Montevideo

bomb exploded in the hall in Munich where he was speaking on 8th November 1939, but turned out to be a carefully arranged Gestapo plot to enable him to say 'Now I am certain! The fact that I left the hall before the Communist bomb exploded is a corroboration that Providence intends me to reach my goal'. Providence intended nothing of the sort, as we now know; but the opposition among the generals was stiffened by the event. By that time, though, Hitler had ordered that the attack in the West should begin on 12th November.

It did not so begin. The Führer was cunning enough to allow himself to accept the advice of his army Commander-in-chief, Walter von Brauchitsch, and Franz Halder, his Chief-of-Staff, to delay the attack because of the winter weather. He saw that by doing so he would later be able to throw their incompetence in their faces and use it to justify his refusal to be influenced by them any further. Though he pretended to accept their

advice, a winter attack in the West did not accord with his intuition, in spite of the urgency with which he had pressed for it. His megalomania was becoming intense and had been fed by the sweeping success in Poland. He was determined to see another débâcle. And with Britain still hurriedly preparing for a war her negligent attitude had ensured would overtake her, there could be no débâcle. Regulars, Territorials and conscripts forming the BEF were still lacking arms and equipment when war was declared. As they arrived in France and took up defensive positions along the Maginot Line and the Belgian frontier, it was clear to Hitler that they were scarcely worth the effort of an all-out attack. But in Britain conscription and training were proceeding more or less smoothly and production of war material was getting into its stride. By the spring there would be on the continent of Europe a British force worthy of defeat. He could afford to wait. 'It may

st me a million men', he told Ernst
eizäcker, Secretary in the Foreign
fice, 'but it will cost the enemy that
o – and the enemy cannot stand it'.
Meanwhile, his most effective blows
uld be aimed at sea power; so
roughout the winter of 1939-40 – the
riod that by its inactivity became
lled 'the phoney war' – it was the
ιvy that did the fighting. The pocket
ttleship *Graf Spee* sank nine British
erchantmen before she was brought
battle on 13th December and
rsued to the River Plate, where she
ιttled herself. Earlier, German
bmarines had sunk the Battleship
yal Oak* in Scapa Flow, and the
med merchant cruiser *Rawalpindi*
d been sunk in battle against the
harnhorst and *Gneisenau* in Novem-
r. But even at sea there were no
ectacular engagements. 'It seems as
he rape of Poland has knocked both
es into shocked inanition', one of
e neutral newspapers of the Irish
public said with surprising credulity
d dubious semantics.

Hitler's 'inanition' was by no means
shocked. Nor was it inanition. He was
carefully planning an operation which
he saw as essential if the western
powers were to be completely defeated
– the invasion of Norway.

That design was one of the out-
standing examples of his generalship.
To control the long Norwegian coast
with its innumerable harbours and
fjords would give him naval and
aircraft bases for attacks against
Allied shipping in the North Atlantic.
To counteract those attacks, British
and French sea and air forces would
have to be drawn off from other vital
areas – for example the Mediterranean
and North Sea; and Hitler was particularly interested in the vulnerability
of the Mediterranean, since to
dominate it was to open the gateway
to French possessions in North Africa.
There was also to be considered the
great material advantage of gaining
control of Norway's immense output
of iron ore. Denied to the enemy, the
lack of that vital commodity could

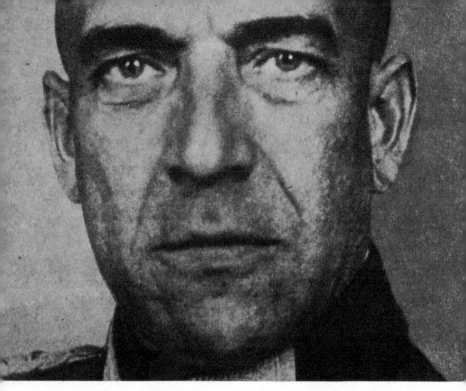

The Norwegian campaign. *Above:* Falkenhorst, the German commander. *Right:* Infantry advance outside Oslo

make a significant difference to their armaments production.

The conception of the Norwegian campaign was claimed by Hitler as his own. True, the German naval archives reveal that Admiral Raeder suggested, at a conference on 10th October 1939, that the capture of Norwegian bases would enable him to challenge British naval supremacy; but 'the Führer cast the suggestion aside furiously' – a reaction that was psychologically in key. He was responding characteristically to the attempted wrenching from him by one of his High Command of a cherished idea. It was a brilliant idea and Hitler knew it. He did not intend to let any credit for it elude him. He took it as an affront that Raeder should innocently have come up with an idea that was already, so to speak, in the portfolio of his intuitive design for the conduct of the war. To cast Raeder's suggestion furiously aside was therefore merely the blustering attempt of a man of un-stable temperament, caught off his

guard, to prevent the reins of contr being taken from his hands.

'Before I became Chancellor', had said to justify his arrogation supreme power, 'I thought the Gener Staff was like a mastiff which had be held tight by the collar becau it threatened all and sundry. Sin then I have to recognize that t General Staff is anything but that. has consistently tried to impede eve action I have thought necessary. is I who have always had to goad this mastiff'.

The General Staff were for the tin being kept completely in the da about the Norwegian operation, sin he could hardly reject Raeder's su gestion and then be seen to adopt it. was in fact unnecessary that the should know. 'Why should I demora ize my enemy by military means if can do so better and more cheap

other ways?' Hitler had written in *Mein Kampf*. The 'other ways' were, in the case of Norway, the establishment of Vidkun Quisling's Fifth Column of Nazi sympathizers. 'Hitler knew', Major-General Fuller has said, that in a democratic country an army is next to useless should the people sympathize with the enemy ... which is why in autocratically ruled countries their governments raise two armies, one to fight their enemies and the other to control their peoples'.

Quisling, like Hitler, was a bitter and fearful opponent of Communism and had, so to speak, prostrated himself before the German leader. His obeisances were not without self-interest. He hoped to carve out a career as Führer of Norway. The party he had formed to follow him, which he called *Nasjonal Samling* (National Unity), had been contemptuously treated by the electorate and gained only two per cent of the votes and no seat in the parliament. Secretly dismayed by that response

he had nonetheless used his army connexions – he was a major and had been Military Attaché in Moscow – to disseminate Nazi ideas among the forces. Those attempts had had considerable success: Hitler's ceaseless drumming up of the military virtues of the Nordic races had not been without its propaganda effect.

So, when the war began, Quisling went to see Hitler in Berchtesgaden to discuss the affairs of the Thule Society, an organization which used Nordic mythology as a cover for its surreptitious political activities. The affairs discussed on this occasion were the tactics of the *Nasjonal Samling*. Hitler himself wrote down what were to be that Party's aims. These were: to restrict British naval power by establishing naval and air bases on the west coast of Norway; to lie athwart the sea communications between Britain and Northern Russia; to open the North Sea and the Atlantic to the German fleet; and to secure the sea route for the shipping of iron ore to Germany. Quisling's help in these undercover activities was to be rewarded with leadership of the Norwegian government as soon as the invasion had proved successful. (His ultimate reward was to have Hitler's memorandum produced in evidence against him at his trial for treason in October 1945.)

Having indulged in a great deal of mutual soft-soaping, Führer and quasi-Führer parted. Hitler had recognized in his henchman a strain of megalomania. It was of a lesser virulence than his own and therefore could be twisted into subservience; but it must be watched. 'Quisling', he later told Himmler, 'must be discredited as soon as he has served his purpose. In no circumstances must he be allowed power of other than secondary value'. For the time being, though, the carrot was before the donkey – a Trojan donkey who could safely be left to organize half the battle for Norway.

Thus, quite apart from Hitler' reluctance to allow any real strategi power to fall into the hands of hi General Staff, it was in the case of th Norwegian campaign unnecessary. A that was needed in Germany was th intensive training of Austrian troop in mountain warfare, and that wa put in hand immediately, their com mander, General von Falkenhorst being given only the sketchiest notio of the venue of his forthcomin expedition – though as an experience soldier he can hardly have been bere of ideas on that subject.

Meanwhile, Hitler continued t prevaricate, and to seem to allo himself to be influenced by the Hig Command and General Staff, whos insistent advice was to delay th attack in the West.

Meanwhile also, the Russians ha set about invading Finland with vast superiority of numbers whic they gleefully assumed would brin that tiny country to her knees in

atter of days and give her mighty onqueror the port of Hangö for a ıval base, which Russia dearly ınted. There was no easy conquest owever. Superior though the ussians were in numbers – they had hundred divisions against the Finns' ıree – they were unbelievably in- ımpetent in organization and rategy. The Finns' resistance – ıey were led by Field-Marshal ınnerheim – kept the enemy at bay ım 30th November 1939 to 10th March 40 and inflicted grievous losses on ıe Russian forces. In the end it was mply brute force, the indiscriminate ırowing into battle of thousands of ussian troops and airmen, that made ınland surrender to Marshal Timo- ınko's hordes. Great noises of ıf-righteous triumph were voiced ıroad in the party organ *Pravda*, but

it was clear that Russian morale had been lowered to near zero by a cam- paign that had been extended, by the Finns' superiority, from the expected three days to more than three months.

To no-one was it more clear than Hitler. Brooding upon his declared intention 'to crush the Soviet Union', he confided to Keitel, his Chief of Staff, that 'the moral defeat of Com- munist Russia at the hands of a tiny country like Finland proves un- equivocally that she stands no chance at all against the organized might of the Reich'. In the circumstances it was a reasonable judgement. But, as he was to find to his cost, he had not taken into account the fact that more effective lessons are learned from defeats than from victories. The Russians learned theirs in Finland.

The period of the phoney war ended in April 1940 with the rapid and complete success of the Norwegian invasion. Quisling's Fifth Column methods proved invaluable. His trait-

The Russo-Finnish war of 1939. Soviet troops occupy Viborg, October 1939

ors occupied Oslo and aided the German airborne troops who landed there. Seaborne troops were stowed into the holds of merchant vessels which sailed up the Kattegat to Oslo to complete the occupation of the capital. Denmark was invaded on the same day (9th April) and capitulated without resistance, having been given a pledge by Hitler that her political independence would be respected. (Needless to say, it wasn't.) By nightfall all the key points of Norway – Oslo, Kristiansund, Trondheim, Bergen, Stavanger – were in Falkenhorst's hands.

The campaign was seen by many in Britain to be an act of madness. Churchill – at that time First Lord of the Admiralty – said, 'I consider that Hitler's action in invadir Scandinavia is as great a strateg and political error as that which wa committed by Napoleon in 1807 whe he invaded Spain . . . I feel that we a: greatly advantaged by what ha occurred, provided we turn to t utmost profit the strategic blunde into which our mortal enemy has bee provoked.'

Far from turning the occasion the utmost profit, delays and mudd resulted in nothing more than tl heroic but useless attempt to wre power from the Germans by combine sea and air attacks on the ports Trondheim, Aandalsnes, Narvik ar Namos. These did not begin till 15t April, by which time the enemy wa firmly rooted in all key centres. any case the naval and air force efforts were so poorly integrated tha the landing of troops in the fjor

and let us have done with you. In the name of God, go!' Two days later Chamberlain resigned and Churchill became Prime Minister. That much at least had been achieved.

It now became very clear that far from being an act of madness Hitler's first blow since the declaration of war had been timed perfectly. For it was followed almost immediately by his second. 'The morning of 10th May dawned', Churchill recorded in his history of the war, 'and with it came tremendous news. Boxes with telegrams poured in from the Admiralty, the War Office, and the Foreign Office. The Germans had struck their long-awaited blow. Holland and Belgium were both invaded. Their frontiers had been crossed at numerous points. The whole movement of the German army upon the invasion of the Low Countries and of France had begun.'

Hitler's 'justification' for pouring his armies into Belgium and Holland was, as before, 'to prevent the clear intention of Britain and France to invade defenceless territory'. His timing continued to be perfect. There was now, in France, a BEF worth attacking. It consisted of seven regiments of light tanks, a regiment of armoured cars of antiquated design, two battalions of infantry tanks (their 'armament' was a single machine gun), and thirteen infantry divisions of which three could scarcely be counted since they had no artillery to support them and only vestigial transport to move them. The BEF's entire backing from the air was from one fighter and one bomber wing of the Royal Air Force, and its lines of communication were excessively long, stretching as they did to Le Havre, Brest and Nantes. The fighting quality of the Force lay almost entirely in its men. Its armour was feeble almost to the point of uselessness; it was underequipped and vulnerable to air attack. But its defeat would be a punishing blow to the Allies.

Hitler also had, as he very well

ould not be accomplished quickly nough, and German bombing attacks ould not be dealt with by British ghters because all the aerodromes ere in German hands. (A crazy cheme to land a Squadron of planes n a frozen lake near Dombaas ended nevitably in their destruction.) The ttempt having been doomed from the art, the Allied Supreme War Council ook themselves like shaggy dogs nd decided to withdraw all troops om central Norway on 27th April, aving a sprinkling in the north to eal with Narvik.

The lamentable conduct of the orwegian affair resulted in the oicing in Westminster of the opinion f the country in general when r L S Amery quoted Cromwell's ords to the Long Parliament: 'You ave sat too long here for any good ou have been doing. Depart, I say,

t: Churchill, as First Lord of the Admiralty, in nautical rig. *Above:* Norwegians
ending Narvik. *Below:* After the British bombardment of Narvik

Manstein, author of the German plan for the invasion of France

Gamelin, French Commander-in-Chief

knew, the French armies to contend with. There were 102 divisions. Forty of them were stretched out from the English Channel to the Maginot Line; twenty-six were in the Line itself; and thirty-six were lined up facing the Alpes Maritimes. They had of course been there all the time. It was a complete mystery to the German General Staff that they had not moved since the war began. General Siegfried Westphal says in *The German Army in the West:*

'Every expert serving at that time [September 1939] in the Western Army felt his hair standing on end when he considered the possibility of an immediate French attack. It was incomprehensible that no such attack should take place, that the appalling weakness of the German defence should be unknown to the French leaders. If the French had thrown the weight of their forces into an offensive in September 1939 they would have been able to reach the Rhine in two weeks. The German forces immediately available in the West were much too weak to block the path of a French assault or even threaten seriously the flanks of the attacking wedge. Naturally units could have been withdrawn rapidly from Poland and transferred

to the West, but nevertheless t French and British air forces sho have found it possible to damage t lines of communication inside G many sufficiently to slow down t process. The theme of every Gene Staff exercise . . . had been the beati off of a French attack by the Germ Army of which parts had to be tained in the East because of . Poland. In each of these exercises t French broke out of the narrow spa of less than two hundred kilometr between the Mosel and the Rhi later proceeding along the northe bank of the Mosel and finally crossi the Upper Rhine in the region Karlsruhe. In every case they had be able to penetrate to the Rhine in t course of a few weeks, even though was assumed that a much great number of divisions, and in particul the majority of the active ones, we taking part in the German defence

Though it was incomprehensible the German General Staff that attack had been made by the Alli in September, it was no mystery Hitler. He had contemptuously w ched the exercises that were based the premise of a French breakthrou at Karlsruhe and remarked to Jo chief of the Wehrmacht control sta

he French were obsessed with dence in 1920; they are obsessed with dence still. They are like a rabbit facing
stoat; they cannot move for fear.'
His own army, he considered, seemed
be fatally conventional. 'I have the
eatest contempt for orthodoxy when
can lead only to feeble ideas. The
neral Staff will strangle themselves
th their orthodoxy'. He had been
lling to let them do so between the
tumn of 1939 and the spring of 1940,
cepting their excuses for delaying
e attack in the West with a pretend-
. patience that conveniently dis-
ised his alarm that his intuition
out the spinelessness of the French
ight be wrong. But he was not
rong. 'The side which stays within
s fortifications is beaten.' Now that
 had secured Norway with an
ipeccably performed set-piece, the
ench had certified themselves as
bby and stupid, and the British had
 usual pushed their Expeditionary
rce over to France with great
nscientiousness and no apparent
ject – now was the time to trigger
 the plan that had been in the
aking throughout the winter. Hence
e spate of dispatches that astonished
r Churchill – and everybody else,
emingly – on the morning of 10th May.
There were two Commands between
tler and his forces: his own, the
KW, Supreme Command of all the
med Forces, and the OKH, the
dinary Army High Command. This
st was the computer that worked
t the details of his grand designs.
e OKH's original plan for attack in
e West was, as Hitler had said,
uninspired. It was to repeat the
erman action of 1914, with a right
ng sweeping movement through
lgium and Holland, a centre op-
site the Ardennes, and a left wing
cing what was now the Maginot
ne. The result would have been
tirely predictable, since the French
so would have been thinking in
rst World War terms – had in fact
sed their plan, such as it was, on
at very method of attack.

**Paul Reynaud, French Prime Minister, on
the eve of war**

An alternative scheme had been
worked out and proposed by Field-
Marshal von Rundstedt's Chief of Staff,
General von Manstein. He thought
that the main thrust should be made
through the Ardennes, since that area
was weakly defended – the French be-
lieving in their innocence that it was
too densely forested for tanks to
operate in. Hitler at once saw the
possibilities of such a plan; but as
with Raeder's proposal for Norway he
had no intention of appearing to be
malleable in the hands of his generals.
It was February before he allowed himself to be 'persuaded'; but thenceforth
he implemented the scheme relent-
lessly, in the face of such opposition
as the OKH put forward on the ground
that it was too risky. He not only
ordered its implementation but –
repeating his behaviour with Raeder –
adopted it as his own. 'My plan will
result in a lightning victory', he told
Halder at the conference on the
morning of 9th May when the final
order to begin the attack – there had
been sixteen earlier orders and count-
ter-orders – was given.

He can scarcely be said to have been
unwarrantably optimistic. By the
afternoon of the 10th Holland was
overrun. 'The Dutch Ministers were

Above: The 'impenetrable' Maginot line falls to the Germans. *Right:* Hitler and Göring gleeful after the defeat of France

in my room', Churchill writes. 'Haggard and worn, with horror in their eyes, they had just flown over from Amsterdam. Their country had been attacked without the slightest pretext of warning. The avalanche of fire and steel had rolled across the frontiers, and when resistance broke out and the Dutch frontier guards fired an overwhelming onslaught was made from the air. The whole country was in a state of wild confusion. The long-prepared defence scheme had been put into operation; the dykes were opened, the waters spread far and wide. But the Germans had already crossed the outer lines, and were now streaming down the banks of the Rhine and through the inner Gravelines defences.'

Two days later the main thrust – forty-four divisions, including a column of armour over a hundred miles long – crossed the Ardennes and the French frontier and were over the River Meuse on the 13th. Its advance was phenomenally quick. There was virtually nothing to oppose it but a couple of divisions of second-rate

French troops, elderly reservists wl were more or less immobile for lack transport and had only one anti-ta gun per kilometre of front. Along tl whole line Louvain – Namur – Dinan Sedan, where the rest of the Frenc Ninth Army had been deployed, battle developed in which the Frenc troops were liquidated by the a vancing tanks of General von Klei and the wickedly effective div bombing of Göring's Stukas. Gener Gamelin, who was the Commander-i Chief of all the Allied armies sent dumbfounded message to Churchill: am surprised and alarmed at the spee and power of the enemy's advance Pathetic creature. He had eve reason to be alarmed. His 'Plan D' ha been designed to face a German attac in September 1939, when the bulk the German army was engaged Poland. It had not been altere one whit in the eight months sinc

Preis 20 ₰

5. Dezember 1

Nummer 49 / 15.

Druck und Verlag
DuMont Schauber
Auslandspreise siehe Fuß der

Kölnische
Illustrierte Zeitung

de
Sieg!

veröffent
Führers
nach der
...ation

cause la
... Eid
repr...
...Marschal, da
...apres la
la France

Left and *above:* Victorious Germans pass the Arc de Triomphe, Paris, May 1940

despite the frequent observations of the British Chiefs of Staff that the German army was growing in strength every day and that its tactics would not necessarily be those of 1914. Gamelin was an out-dated old buffer who had been expected to retire on the outbreak of war and hand over command of the French and British armies to General Georges. He could not bear to relinquish his authority, however; and now that his rickety arrangements had proved disastrous he came bleating to Churchill for help – 'Ten more squadrons of fighters'.

Churchill had no fighters to give him. On the morning of the 15th the French Prime Minister, Paul Reynaud, telephoned him reproachfully. 'We have been defeated. We are beaten. We have lost the battle'. Churchill could not believe it. He promised to

y to Paris and talk, rather as a
arent comforts a terrified child in a
orm. He arrived at the Quai d'Orsay
t 5.30 the same afternoon. His first
ords to Gamelin after he had heard a
in-down of the situation and under-
ood the sinister significance of the
rdennes breakthrough were: 'Where
 the strategic reserve?' Gamelin re-
lied that there was none. Thinking
e had misunderstood the question
hurchill put it in French. *'Ou est la
asse de manoeuvre?'* And again
amelin replied, *'Aucune'*.

Now it was Churchill's turn to be
umbfounded. 'What were we to think
f the great French Army and its
ighest chiefs? It had never occurred
 me that any commanders having
 defend five hundred miles of en-
aged front would have left themselves
nprovided with a strategic reserve.
o-one can defend with certainty so
ide a front; but when the enemy has
ommitted himself to a major thrust
hich breaks the line one can always
ave, one *must* always have, a mass
f divisions which marches up in
igorous counterpoint at the moment
hen the first fury of the offensive has
ent its force.

'What was the Maginot Line for? It
hould have economized troops upon
 large section of the frontier, not only
ffering many sally-ports for local
ounter-strokes, but also enabling
irge forces to be held in reserve; and
his is the only way these things can
e done. But now there was no re-
erve. I admit this was one of the
reatest surprises I have had in my life.
hy had I not known more about it,
ven though I had been so busy at
he Admiralty? Why had the British
overnment, and the War Office above
ll, not known more about it?'

He might well have asked. Two
ears later the same baffled Churchill
as to ask the same question about
he lack of defences in Singapore. The
imple answer in both cases was that

he Pact of Steel. Sometimes it nearly
ollapsed

he assumed, mistakenly, that those
responsible were fit for their jobs. The
enemy knew better.

Hitler's prophecy of a lightning
victory was fulfilled. Within a month
the tremendous impetus of the
German advance had resulted, *seriatim*,
in the surrender of Holland, the
surrender of Belgium, the evacuation
from Dunkirk of 337,131 men of the
BEF who had been trapped between
Rundstedt's forces advancing from the
south and General von Bock's advancing from the north, and the
German occupation of Paris. The
French Government fled to Bordeaux
on 14th June. The aged Marshal
Pétain succeeded Reynaud as head of
the Government and his immediate
task was to seek an armistice. It was
the end of the Third Republic.

The Führer managed the armistice
with a stroke of malicious drama. He
ordered that it should be signed in the
famous railway sleeping-car in which
the 1918 armistice had been signed.
The car stood as a museum piece at
Réthondes in the Forest of Compiègne
beside the stone on which was en-
graved the memorial 'Here on the
eleventh of November 1918 succumbed
the criminal pride of the German
empire, vanquished by the free peoples
which it tried to enslave.' William
Shirer, the War Correspondent, who
was present, says, 'To dictate an
armistice in this historic place was
sweet revenge for the man who had
been a lowly corporal in the army
which had been forced to give up in
1918, and he did not hide his feelings.
Standing a few feet away, I saw his
face light up, successively, with hate,
scorn, revenge, triumph . . .'

For a few moments he stood thus in
the coach; then he marched out into
the sunny clearing, leaving Keitel to
read the preamble to the declaration –
a declaration that Hitler himself had
written, and which was 'to efface once
and for all by an act of reparative
justice a memory . . . which was
resented by the German people as the
greatest shame of all time'.

General Keitel, for once, answers Hitler back

Lest it be assumed that Hitler watched with icy calm or tranquil smile as his armies swept through Europe, let that impression be corrected at once. Hitler was no Wellington – though like the great General of Waterloo, his army leaders had so far proved to be better than his opponents'. But their quality owed nothing whatever to him. Nor did he exactly encourage their tolerance.

Throughout his infamous career from nonentity to Führer of the Third Reich there had been stormy scenes whenever events fell out badly or his generals ran counter to him in their proposals, and often when they didn't. His petulance was sometimes masked by a deceptive oiliness – 'the smile on the face of the tiger' – when he planned the obliteration of anyone who threatened to undermine his authority. (He had invited Röhm to tea on the afternoon of 4th June 1934 and was 'excessively cheerful and friendly' while planning the purge of the 30th, : which Röhm was shot after receivir a letter from the Führer thanking hi for his 'imperishable services'.) B all his generals testify in their diarie and other records to the scenes rage that so frequently formed th backdrop to the 'conferences' at whic the schemes of war were propounde Halder, for example, on 18th May 194

'Führer keeps worrying about sout flank. He rages and screams that w are on the way to ruin the who campaign. He won't have any part i continuing the operation in a wes ward direction'.

And, earlier, Weizäcker on the ev of war:

'He grew more and more excited ar began to wave his arms as he shoute in my face:

'"If England wants to fight for year, I shall fight for a year; if Englar wants to fight two years I shall fig] two years." He paused and the yelled, his voice rising to a shri scream and his arms milling wildl: "If England wants to fight for thr ears I shall fight for three years." he movements of his body now began to follow those of his arms, and when e finally bellowed "And if necessary will fight for ten years" he brandished is fist and bent down so that it early touched the floor. The situation as highly embarrassing, so embarrassing in fact that Göring reacted erceptibly to the spectacle Hitler as making of himself by turning on is heel so that he had his back to oth of us.'

That outburst – very typical – was merely Hitler's response to a suggestion by Weizäcker that England might be readier to fight than he had ontemptuously implied.

There were occasions too when ewilderment seemed to overcome im as he contemplated the inevitable esults of his actions, as if an unfair low had been struck at him by fate. ne such occasion was the reading to im, by his interpreter Paul Schmidt, f the British ultimatum on the orning of 3rd September 1939. chmidt writes:

'Hitler was sitting at his desk and ibbentrop stood by the window. oth looked up expectantly as I came . I stopped at some distance from itler's desk, and then slowly transted the British Government's ultiatum. When I finished there was omplete silence. Hitler sat immobile, azing before him. He was obviously a loss, as was afterward stated, but e did not rage as others allege. He sat ompletely silent and unmoving. After n interval, which seemed an age, he urned to Ribbentrop, who had reained standing by the window. What now?" asked Hitler with a vage look, as though implying that is Foreign Minister had misled him out England's probable reaction.'

Throughout the voluminous docuentation that comments on his beaviour there is abundant evidence of is instability. It is an extension and agnification of August Kubizek's ecognition of the same characteriic. But now his manic-depressive nature had been intensified by the action of *Spirochaeta pallida* on the cortex of his brain and possibly exacerbated by the drugs used to combat the disease. 'It is remarkable', Göebbels wrote in his diary in January 1940 with an unwitting finger on the heart of the matter, 'how much the Führer is becoming an enlargement of himself.'

Not only is there a veritable cornucopia of documentation of Hitler's increasing instability, but also of his militant determination to interfere with the plans of the Army High Command. Only in the Polish campaign can he be said to have left his Generals to plan and execute in detail a conquest that turned out to be triumphant. Perhaps their triumph was too much for him. From the beginning of the Norwegian campaign his megalomania forced, as Westphal says, a gulf between him 'and the German army leaders [that] was absolute and unbridgeable. It arose from the always irreconcilable conflict between concrete and abstract thinking, between sober objectivity and the chasing of fancies, between logical calculation based on facts and the attempt to force the facts to fit impossible desires . . . In the Third Reich the motto was "Death to the expert, particularly the soldier". Not only Hitler but almost every Party leader believed himself to possess a more soundly based judgement in all questions concerning the conduct of the war than that possessed by the leaders of the Army.'

The general can be allowed his bitterness. He was a staff officer of great distinction under Rundstedt, Kesselring and Rommel and was no dyed-in-the-wool reactionary. He saw Hitler set blood 'flowing in rivers without scruple' and recognized his foolish fear of letting the smallest control slip from his fingers as another manifestation of his instability:

'His experience was the common one of dilettanti. For a certain time they have beginner's luck; they turn out to be right where the experts were wrong; in their audacity they achieve much that the professionals could not have brought about with the same speed and ease. Then, however, in the intoxication of success, their feet leave the common ground. This happens in all walks of life and it is no different in warfare. The military layman underestimates the strength of the enemy and rates his own potentialities too highly. He sees things not as they are but as he would like to have them. He drives away all who would warn him, lest they should cast shadows over his rosy picture, and he will have none of their advice. But when the dilettante is not an average man whose absurdity is soon made apparent, but a being who holds absolute power in his hands and who is driven by demonic urges, it is far worse. For then as time goes on he rejects even that truth which he once had recognized. Even so was it with Hitler.'

There is a measure of understandable misjudgement here. To the professional all who lack his trained skill are amateurs. The 'natural' is unacceptable, his intuitions are not to be trusted. If Hitler had attained a command in the First World War he would have been, so to speak, eligible for consideration in the hierarchy; if such a command had been even in the slightest degree noteworthy he would have been acceptable; for his rantings about the 'Masonry' of the Army were not wholly unjustified. Soldiering, in Germany as in England, had always, until the inter-war period, suffered from the effects of class structure –an effect good in some ways, disastrous in others; but ineradicable. 'Soldiers', Hitler once told Goebbels,'learn seven principles of war like a creed. They are certain that so long as they maintain the objective, keep up offensive action, surprise the enemy, economize with their forces, make good security arrangements, co-operate with their flanking formations, and concentrate on conquest, they are bound to win.

They forget that the enemy knows th same formula. They forget tha battles can be half won before a sho is fired. They forget the value of th political weapon.'

But by the time of the fall of Franc Hitler had forced all possible advant age from the political weapon. B trick, propaganda and diplomacy h had secured his followers and hi allies. (Mussolini quaveringly thre in his hand with his fellow Fascis on 10th June 1940.) The German natio was behind him – in effect in its er tirety, since the Gestapo, the cor centration camp and the firing squa awaited those who demurred or wai dered from the ideological fold wher Hitler was bellwether. He had no mor to gain from the hypnotism of hi presence at such gatherings as th Nuremberg rallies. The cunning of the politician needed to be tempere by the discipline of the soldier; bt that was not a quality so easil wrung from a man of Hitler's stamp.

The question naturally arises, ther as to his ability as a military leade Was his 'intuition', his psychologica insight into his opponents' reaction a valuable asset? His generals, drive frantic by his interference – unles they were virtually no more tha toadying personal assistants lik Jodl and Keitel – would have set littl store by it. The harsh realities military manoeuvres were to the far more important than any asses ment of the character of their opp nents. It was, for army men, reasonable order of priorities. It d not follow, however, that it was ip facto the right order. Used wisely, th gift of insight is of immense value i supplementing, if not instigating, course of action. But a serious fla lay in Hitler's inability to subjuga it to the commonsense dictates military prerogative. It was a fla that was to have fatal effects on h leadership.

The General in decline

Before pursuing the track of Hitler's Generalship from its zenith to its nadir, it will be as well to summarize and evaluate his achievements to date.

His first step to military power was of course to acquire theoretical overlordship of all the armed forces at the same time as he united the offices of President and Chancellor in August 1934, upon the death of Hindenberg. (This titular office of Supreme Commander was indivisible from that of Head of State.) He found, though, that he had acquired also a hornet's nest of disruptive forces. The reactionary spirit of the Officer Corps was one he was well aware of. He had seen many signs of sullen objection to his attitude to the Church, to the speed with which he was insisting on rearmament and conscription, to dangerous moves such as the reoccupation of the Rhineland, and to the infiltration of Himmler's police methods into the cherished traditions of the Corps. But there were smaller irritants that he quickly realized could be equally trouble-

some to him; and those he shrewd[ly] turned to advantage as soon as oppo[r]tunities presented themselves.

In particular, the personal affairs [of] General Werner von Blomberg, W[ar] Minister and Commander-in-Chief [of] all the Armed Forces, and Colone[l] General Werner von Fritsch, Com[m]ander-in-Chief of the Army, prove[d] to be an Open Sesame on the Führe[r's] route through the labyrinth of power[.]

Blomberg was a weak man who h[ad] achieved high rank in the army on[ly] because he greased palms and ma[de] genuflections in the right direction [at] the right time. He had no speci[al] military ability. He had wormed h[is] way into President Hindenberg['s] favour and had been nominated W[ar] Minister as a condition of Hitler['s] appointment to the Chancellorship [in] 1933. Hitler had expected him to [be] something of a thorn in his side; b[ut]

Map conference with Rundstedt. Hitler dismissed him no less than three times

as things turned out Blomberg had, by his vacillating nature, been a valuable link between the upstart Chancellor and the rigidly reactionary Officer Corps. Hitler, in 1933 altogether uncertain of holding on to the power he had achieved largely by chance, shrewdly cultivated the acquaintance of the man who could chamfer away the Army's resentment.

Then, at the end of 1937, Blomberg decided to get married and asked Hitler to act as a witness at the wedding. Himmler, however, had looked into the affianced lady's past. The search had proved rewarding. Heydrich, Himmler's chief of intelligence had produced a dossier recording forty-two convictions for prostitution against Fraülein Erna Grühn. Even more titillating was a file of obscene photographs for which the War Minister's intended had posed. Himmler arranged for a surreptitious leakage of this interesting information and also brought it to Hitler's attention. The Führer, genuinely outraged by Blomberg's indiscretion and his seeming endorsement of the liaison, insisted upon the War Minister's resignation.

His natural successor was the Army Commander-in-Chief, Fritsch, but Hitler's and Himmler's long-term interests demanded that the automatic succession of generals to War Ministry should cease. It was therefore very convenient that the Gestapo was able to produce an even more damaging dossier against Fritsch, which portrayed him as a practising homosexual. He also produced a male prostitute who had been bribed or bullied into identifying Fritsch as a former client. All this was a farrago of his (the evidence in fact related to a retired Captain Frisch, as Himmler and the Gestapo well knew) but the atmosphere of crisis robbed Frisch's explanations of conviction. He was sent on leave and though eventually cleared by a Court of Honour, never reinstated.

Having thus removed two obstacles

from his path Hitler announced to th Cabinet on 4th February that h himself would now become Com mander-in-Chief of all the Arme Forces. That is, he assumed Suprem Command in a practical as well as titular sense. The War Minist would be abolished and its pla taken by the OKW – the *Oberkomman der Wehrmacht*, or High Commar of all the Armed Forces, with t yes-man General Wilhelm Keitel its administrative head and at Hitler right hand. Brauchitsch would made Commander-in-Chief of t Army, Göring would be a Fiel Marshal and the senior officer of the forces, and more than a doze other generals of whose loyalty Hitl was extremely doubtful would transferred to the retired list.

Thus, by way of events that he h not even precipitated himself, Hitl undermined the power of the Offic Corps and by the same token ensur that he was actual as well as titul director of all the armed forces. T Head of State, moving warily, h reinforced his power as dictator wi those of general. That was his mo valuable achievement, since without none of his later ones could have be attempted, let alone implemented.

There followed in the autumn that same year, 1938, the omino seizure of the Sudetenland – mora assisted by the Allies, which made perhaps, a second-rate achievemen and, a year later still, the brillia political stroke of the agreeme with the Soviet Union that held t Russians at bay while Poland w dealt with in a campaign in whic for the last time, Hitler's genera were left alone to make their ov plans. The political experiment of war localized to Poland failed, but t military one of non-interference the professionals' strategy was t successful for Hitler's increasi megalomania and determined him plan and direct future campaig himself. It was a grave error.

Norway, though, hid its effects f

...er's variant, 'Barbarossa': the capture of Leningrad is stipulated as essential ...re the subsequent – and conclusive – drive on Moscow

In apparent harmony, Hitler and (right to left) Fritsch, Blomberg and Göring watch manoeuvres

the time being; and when that subtly planned and cheaply accomplished campaign was succeeded by the fall of France and the Low Countries and the débâcle of Dunkirk it was evident – anyway to him – that his own and others' utterances about his being a God-sent saviour, the choice of Providence, et cetera, had been the solemn truth. 'The effect of cerebral syphilis on a nature already afflicted with megalomania', the venereologist Anwyl-Davies has said, 'is always to increase confidence that every kind of opposition can be overcome, to see the path ahead lighted by Messianic triumphs when in fact ruinous disasters lurk in the shadows.'

To Hitler, his next step was clear. He did not underestimate the British characteristic of dogged resistance; nor did he mistakenly assume that his enemy would easily submit to the humiliation of Dunkirk. 'They turn and snap like terriers', he t Brauchitsch. Brauchitsch sharply minded him that Rundstedt's enc ling armour, ordered to cut off destroy the British forces heading Dunkirk, had been stopped by Hitl own last-minute command from c pleting their task. Furiously, Hi dared Brauchitsch to question wisdom of his direction. From heart of the storm of abuse Brau itsch grasped the notion that Hi had deliberately intended the Brit to escape from Dunkirk so that chances of suing for peace with th could be improved. This may b been Hitler's vague intention begin with; but in fact it was Rundst himself who pointed out to Hitler t it was 'necessary to save the arm for further operations' and stopped the encirclement movem with the Führer's agreement. Hi was therefore right to expect escaped enemy to 'turn and s like terriers'.

All the same, he evidently had a
if conviction that there might be
approach for peace, for on 21st May,
en the continuing withdrawal of
itish forces made their retreat to
e sea (or their annihilation in
ndstedt's pincer grip) virtually cer-
n, Hitler had warned Admiral
eder that the Navy's plan for the
asion of Britain 'was exceptionally
ficult and must in any case be
elved' while he considered 'more
gent matters'. Whether those more
gent matters were self-reproaches
permitting the Dunkirk escape or
uses in which he hoped overtures for
ace would fall cannot now be
ablished.
As for the invasion plan, of which
thing whatever had been discussed
any of the Führer's planning con-
ences until now, it was a routine
aft that had been made as soon as
itain had declared war and had been
osing in the German Admiralty
altered ever since. It was no more
an an embryo and had taken no
count of any possibility but that of
straightforward naval fleet bom-
rding the south coast and ferrying
ops across the English Channel at
narrowest point. Raeder's enquiry
21st May had been merely to ascer-
in whether Hitler wanted the plan
veloped in greater detail. A month
er, with no sign of any white flag
pearing on the ramparts of an
battled Britain, Raeder pressed the
estion again, and again Hitler
peared sceptical. He was, however,
re in his own mind that the next
ep must be to mount the invasion.
o doubt his scepticism disguised his
ual reluctance to admit anybody
se's ideas as practical.) His change of
art was confirmed by two directives,
e first issued on 2nd July:
'The Führer has decided that under
rtain conditions – the most im-
rtant of which must be the achieve-
ent of the Luftwaffe's superiority in
e air – an invasion of England may
ke place.'
The second, dated 16th July, said

'Since England in spite of her militarily hopeless position shows no sign
of coming to terms, I have decided to
prepare an invasion plan against
England and if necessary carry it out.
The preparations for this plan must be
completed by mid-August'.

At a conference five days later he
told the army, navy and air force
chiefs that there was a 'possibility of
a change in political relations with
Russia'. (Since the services chiefs
already knew his intentions toward
Russia, which had not changed, this is
a somewhat mystic comment. Presumably he referred to the superficially good relationship with Russia
still extant and implied that it would
not be long before his true intention
was made manifest by invasion in the
East. This would coincide with the
strategical decision to deal with
England first and thus ensure his
ability to concentrate all his forces on
the Russian front.) Because of the
possibility of political change the
invasion of England – code-named
'Sea Lion' – was to be regarded as the
most effective way of concluding the
war in the West first.

'But even though the distance is
short', he warned the services chiefs –
who can scarcely have been surprised
by the information – 'this is the
crossing of a sea that is dominated by
the enemy. It is not a one-crossing
affair, as in Norway; operational
surprise cannot be expected; a defensively prepared and utterly determined enemy faces us and dominates
the sea area we must use. For the
Army forty divisions will be required.
The most difficult part will be the
material reinforcements and stores.
We cannot count on supplies of any
kind being available to us in England.
Nor can we afford anything but complete mastery of the air. And this
must be linked with a full appreciation of the weather situation. The
time of year is the most important
factor, for the weather in the North
Sea and the Channel during the end of
September is bad, and fogs begin by

mid-October. The main invasion must therefore be completed by 15th September.'

The generals had learned to control their resentment when their Führer infuriatingly told them obvious facts that they were paid to know and knew. Similarly they hesitated to tell him, when the time came, that if he wanted his Luftwaffe to attain aerial mastery there was so far no prospect of attaining it in the Battle of Britain.

That attempt at mastery had begun in full force on 10th July and six weeks later had not achieved its object, which, militarily speaking, was the creation of complete confusion in London and the cutting off of all communication with the threatened south coast so that the invasion forces would land in conditions so chaotic that the defenders would stand little chance of survival. Far from achieving mastery of the air, Göring's Luftwaffe was in fact facing disastrous losses; and as August went by and Raeder's

Naval Staff were showing signs edginess because they were unable get on with their protective mi. laying in the Channel without the a cover they had been promised, t. vital co-operation between the thr services diminished. At the same tir doubts about the Channel weath increased. So did .doubts about d feating the Royal Air Force. In shor Hitler had made a tactical blunder l allowing Rundstedt to let the Briti escape at Dunkirk in the hope securing a quick cheap peace; and h generals had mistimed and muddl the follow-up invasion, which : amount of tinkering could now mal successful. The axiom of war that o should always reinforce success b never failure had proved to be true.

By the middle of September 'S

Blomberg. *Below:* **With the service chiefs, Fritsch, Göring and Raeder, he salutes the Führer.** *Right:* **Lined up with Nazi Party worthies, 1937**

Lion' had shrunk to a face-saving threat, as Raeder's report shows:

'The present air situation does not provide conditions for carrying out the operation.

'If "Sea Lion" fails it will mean a great gain in prestige for the British.

'"Sea Lion" however must not yet be cancelled, as the anxiety of the British must be kept up; if cancellation became known it would be a great relief to the British . . . [whose] main units of the Home Fleet are being held in readiness to repel the landing.

The operation remained a vague threat until February 1942, when its dusty files were finally consigned to the archives. However, no-one on either. side seriously believed in it after October 1940. By that time the Battle of Britain had proved a costly failure for Göring's Luftwaffe, and the most quoted phrase in Britain was Churchill's 'Never in the field of human conflict was so much owed by so many to so few'.

Britain having successfully repelled the efforts of the Luftwaffe to reduce the capital to chaos and the rest of the country to submission, and 'Sea Lion' having failed through mismanagement, Hitler lost no time in making new plans. He told his generals of them at a conference which, Halder records, was notable for its calm.

'Our efforts must now be directed to the elimination of all factors that permit England to hope for a change in the situation. Britain's hope lies in Russia and perhaps to some extent in the United States. So, if Russia drops out of the picture, America too is lost to Britain, because the elimination of Russia would greatly increase Japan's power in the Far East. Therefore: Russia's destruction must be made our next aim, and the sooner she is crushed the better. The attack will achieve its purpose only if Russia can be shattered to the roots with one blow. If we start next May [1941] we' will have five months to finish the job.

Hitler, Blomberg and Hess watch a Luftwaffe fly past

At the same time he allowed no other aspect of the war, political or military, to elude his designs. He conferred with General Franco about the possibility of Spain entering the war on Germany's side in exchange for an Axis-conquered Gibraltar, Morocco and Algeria; he got Mussolini's agreement to make no move toward the Balkans in exchange for 'the exclusive right of operations in the Mediterranean sphere'; and he connived with Pétain, who still stood feebly at the head of the defeated French government and was poisonously influenced by Pierre Laval, the traitor of Vichy, to defend the North African colonies with what was left of the French navy against British naval intervention. (France was to be rewarded with colonial possessions after a carve-up of the defeated British Empire.)

He based these designs on sound psychological reasoning. Russia he had continued to think of since the

Finnish campaign as having 'no chance at all against the organized might of the Reich'. Mussolini he despised for his jealousy and fear of falling off the Axis roundabout. Franco he despised for trying to jump on it too late. To Jodl he confided that 'the Duce is acting precisely as I expected in Africa; and his troops too. We have the better part of the bargain in letting him exhaust himself there while we concern ourselves with the Rumanian oil supplies'.

The Duce, living on the glory of his 'conquest' of Abyssinia in 1936 and his crackpot notion of building a new Roman Empire, had begun his campaign in Africa in October 1940 with the blatantly trumpeted success of driving the British defence force of 2,000 out of Somaliland. To do this he had strained every nerve and flung into battle 25,000 of the 500,000 men he had concentrated in Libya, Abyssinia and Somalia. Having completed that triumph he and his Commander-in-Chief, Marshal Graziani, had sat gleefully backslapping each other while the British Navy quietly pushed through the Mediterranean a huge convoy carrying reinforcements to Egypt. With these reinforcements the campaign commander, General Wavell, achieved his great victories at Sidi Barrani and Tobruk and by the middle of January 1941 had humiliatingly defeated the Italian forces and captured 150,000 of them.

At the same time as he began the African campaign Mussolini, finding it impossible to resist interfering in the Balkans, invaded Greece through Albania; and there too the 'victorious Italian troops', as the Duce called them, were put to ignominious flight within a week.

However, pleased though Hitler might be that his despised ally had proved to be so empty of head and so flabby of heart, he was bound to assist him in order to secure German political ends; and in March 1941 one of his most experienced Generals in armoured warfare, Erwin Rommel, attacked and drove Wavell back into Egypt. 'The Führer is of the opinion', Raeder wrote in his diary, 'that it is vital for the outcome of the war that Italy does not collapse . . . It would mean a great loss of prestige for the Axis powers'.

In the Balkans too Hitler had had to assist the Duce. Greece having proved unconquerable by the Italians he had despatched some twenty divisions in early April 1941 with the object of overrunning both Yugoslavia and Greece. His alliance with Mussolini was proving extremely expensive in terms of troops. He was not without reason in his bitter reproaches against 'ungrateful and unreliable friends'.

As for Rumania, he had made his first overt moves in that direction in September 1940 by sending 'military missions [whose] tasks will be to guide friendly Rumania in organizing and instructing her forces. They will have other tasks, which must remain secret to the world, the Rumanians, and our own troops. These will be: to prepare for development from Ruman-

ian bases of German forces in case a war with Soviet Russia is forced upon us, and to protect the oil district.'

The poker-faced qualification 'in case' was somewhat comical in view of Hitler's declared ambitions in the east; but it would not have surprised the Russians, who were already highly suspicious of German intentions in Rumania – and indeed elsewhere. There had been no difficulty about the partition of Poland in 1939; but with Russia and Germany trying to double-cross each other, each clinging to Rumanian oil supplies for future intentions, there was considerable resentment in Moscow when Hitler ordered eight mechanized divisions to stand by to seize the oilfields. It was a false alarm; but its effect was not mitigated by the arrival at the Kremlin of a Top Secret wire that announced that a military alliance between German, Italy and Japan was to be signed on 27th September 1940.

'The alliance', the Berlin wire stated with its hand on its heart, 'is directed exclusively against American warmongers. This is not expressly stated in the terms of the treaty but can be unmistakably inferred from its terms. Its exclusive purpose is to bring the elements pressing for America's entry into the war to their senses by conclusively demonstrating to them that if they enter the present struggle they will automatically have to deal with the three great powers as adversaries.'

This comforting letter was followed by a visit by Stalin's henchman, Molotov, to Berlin. At one of the conferences in the Russian Embassy he was assured that, regardless of American intervention 'no Anglo-Saxon will ever again be allowed to land on the European continent, for England is beaten and it is only a question of time before she admits her defeat'. Somewhat unfortunately the meeting had to be adjourned because of an air raid alarm and Molotov icily enquired, 'If England is defeated, why are we in an air raid shelter with

Himmler whispers pleasantries into Hitler's ear, 1938. His power is growing

British bombs falling?'

The effect of that sarcasm and of Russia's now obvious doubts and suspicions was only to arouse Hitler to uncontrollable furies frequently displayed in daily 'conferences' that should more properly be called harangues. Had Hanisch, Loffner and Neumann, the companions of his early days in Vienna, been present they would wryly have recognized the vastly magnified version of the characteristic they knew so well. His petulant and boring sounding-off about the injustices and inefficiencies of 'the system' had become a psychopathic malady that demanded that everything should be moulded to his will. His outbursts were but the harbingers of his malice against his own army chiefs who dared to guide him, his supposed allies who dared to thwart him, and his enemies who were tougher than he expected.

In spite of the by now clearly defined turn of his mind toward insanity Hitler still had no difficulty in working out the most complex military manoeuvres. But there was a weakness in his psychological appreciations. It was to turn away from circumstantial difficulties that impinged on his intuitive assessments. For example, Franco's hesitation in throwing in his hand with the Axis because he had noted with some dismay a single day's news that Graziani's army had been routed, *HMS Illustrious* had sailed unhindered through the

where, he told Jodl, 'We have only to kick in the door and the whole rotten structure will come tumbling down'.

In its six pages – only nine copies were printed – the directive declares, first, that

'The German Armed Forces must be prepared to *crush Soviet Russia in a quick campaign* before the end of the war against England ... Preparations are to be completed by 15th May 1941 ... The mass of the Russian army in western Russia is to be destroyed in daring operations by driving forward deep armoured wedges, and the retreat of intact, battle-ready troops is to be prevented. The ultimate object of the operation is to establish a defence line against Asiatic Russia from a Line running from the Volga River to Archangel'.

Having stated the objective he went on to explain how attacks were to be launched in the north from Finland and in the south from Rumania. The dividing line between the two attacks would be the Pripet Marshes. One army group would gain possession of the Baltic States and Leningrad and another drive through White Russia and link up with it, trapping the Russian forces retreating from the Baltic. South of the marshes a third army group would advance through the Ukraine to Kiev. Their flank would be protected by Rumanian and German troops in the south who would move toward Odessa and the Black Sea and overrun the industrial concentration in the Donets basin.

It was all very skilful and practical. 'You have nothing to do but work out the details', he told Halder, 'and that you will do by the end of next month [January 1941]. It is vital that no delay should occur. There are vast distances to be dealt with in Russia and the Russian winter is also a deciding factor. The victory must be complete before we are called upon to fight the weather. All my plans are determined by that factor.'

So they may have been. He had not forgotten that both Charles XII and

editerranean to Egypt, and Genoa s being shelled by British warships. t though he might turn away from kward difficulties Hitler could still least make his assessments and lieve unshakeably in their accuracy. uch belief is of course inseparable om megalomania.) Halder records out this time that 'the Führer aims to be *always* right and at the ghtest suggestion otherwise will int to Czechoslovakia, Poland, rway and Cyrenaica – screaming the incompetence of us soldiers d sheltering behind the delusions his egotism.'

If one needs evidence of his strategi- l ability there is no finer example at is time than the famous Directive . 21 outlining 'Barbarossa', his an for the conquest of Russia –

poleon had been defeated by the
im adversary Winter. But he had
tally left out of account another
ctor: his own irrepressible malice
ward those who thwarted him.

The 'military missions' to Rumania
which the Russians were so justi-
bly suspicious, since the Rumanian
ntier adjoins the Ukraine for
me four hundred miles west from
e Black Sea, had by the end of
bruary 1941 been built into a force
nearly three quarters of a million
en. Bulgaria, adjoining Rumania on
e south, had also been inveigled into
tler's grasp with the promise of
cess to the Aegean through an
xis-controlled Greece. The *quid pro
o* would be the occupation of Bul-
ria by German troops and the
nsequent denial of Bulgaria to the
British as a base from which they
could bomb Rumanian oilfields.

Complete control of the Balkans,
however, could not be gained without
co-operation from Yugoslavia; and
Prince Paul, who was ruling as Regent
for the eighteen-year-old King Peter
II, hurriedly and secretly trotted off
with his Prime Minister and Foreign
Minister to Vienna on 25th March as
if they were obsequious puppies ans-
wering the bidding snap of the
Führer's fingers. Without question
they yielded to his demand that
German troops and war material
should be allowed transit through
Yugoslavia, 'though those troops
would at all times respect the sov-
reignty and territorial integrity of
Yugoslavia'. Their prize, they were
told, would be the Greek port of
Salonika 'as soon as I have determined the Greek issue'.

Unfortunately for Hitler the Yugos-
lav people were not so anxious to sell
out their country. While Paul was in
Vienna their fury mounted and they
prepared to overthrow the Regency

Above: Dunkirk, May 1940. Evacuated troops take a last look. Right: Me-110s over London, August 1940

and bring young King Peter to the throne. Paul returned to find an uprising brewing. The Pact he and his Ministers had so obsequiously signed was in effect torn up. The German Ambassador, driving through the streets of Belgrade, was held up by a crowd celebrating the overthrow of the obnoxious régime of Hitler's puppet and the ambassadorial car was spat upon.

It was this insult even more than the ruination of his cunningly organized *coup* that infuriated Hitler. His malice manifested itself in a new military operation that was given first – and, as it turned out, fatal – priority. It was called, with singular lack of subtlety, 'Operation Punishment' and it was planned during and immediately after a meeting at the Chancellery on 27th March 1941 when Hitler was in such a rage that, according to Brauchitsch, 'there was froth on his lips and his clothes turned dark with sweat.' Brauchitsch and Halder attempted to calm him down and even went to the length of summoning the physician

Morell. But he refused to be calme The Reich had been insulted by a intolerable insolence and there w: no question of waiting to see if t young king's new government wou come to heel as the Regent's had.

'Yugoslavia is to be crushed witho mercy', he shouted. It was a repetitio of the fist-banging display tha Weizäcker had recorded in 1939 on much more violent. (The increasing frequent rages and unrestrain violence were typical symptoms of ti progress of syphilis.) 'No diplomat enquiries will be made, no ultimatur will be presented. Yugoslavia will mercilessly destroyed.'

At that stage Halder reminded hi that he had ordered the start 'Barbarossa' in mid-May – only s weeks hence – and that an addition task for the army of the magnitude the complete destruction of a nati would inevitably delay it.

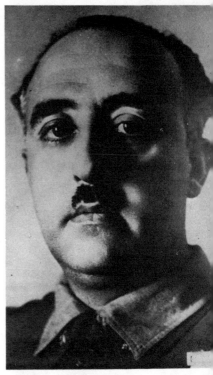

Above Left: Pierre Laval. *Above Right:*
General Franco. *Right:* Battle of Sidi
Birrani, January 1941. Some
of Wavell's 150,000 Italian
prisonners

'Only if I command a delay', Halder
says Hitler told him.

'He was still raging and trembling.
The General Staff stood rigidly in
their places, fearing apoplexy . . .
Morell stood helplessly by . . . Nobody
could see the possibility of diverting
forces for this new campaign; nor
could we see the sense of expending
so much on what was no more than a
spiteful blow.'

It was that of course; but now that
the justification for it had been given
him it at once became more important
– a stretching of his capacity. As
Liddell Hart has said,

'The preparation and contemplation
of vast strategic plans always in-
toxicated him. The doubts which his
generals expressed, when he dis-

osed the trend of his mind, merely erved to make it more definite. Had e not been proved right on each issue here they had doubted his capacity o succeed? He must prove them rong again – and more strikingly. heir doubts showed that for all their ubservience they still had an underring distrust of him as an amateur'.

He did not in fact insist on maintaining the 'Barbarossa' schedule. hough his egomania might demand is refusal to appear to accept any rthodox military advice from his enerals, he could hardly fail to be ware of his numerical inferiority in he matter of tanks compared with the ussians, or of the need for intensive oncentrations of armour in the Balans if he was to achieve quick conest there. Therefore, on 1st April, hen the General Staff were working t the details of the campaign in ugoslavia, he commanded a postonement of the start of 'Barbarossa' om the middle of May to the iddle of June.

So, on 6th April 'Operation Punishment' was launched. Belgrade war bombed to destruction by wave aftes wave of Göring's bombers. Nearly twenty thousand people were killed in that attack alone; and since the country was totally unprepared it surrendered within ten days.

At the same time, the German troops that had been massed in Bulgaria drove over the border into Greece, where Mussolini had met heroic resistance which time and again put his troops to flight. The Greeks had been reinforced by British divisions in March; but these too now were overcome by the huge forces that Hitler drove into the Balkans. (Twenty-eight divisions, including twenty-four that had been diverted from the 'Barbarossa' assembly area in Poland.) Only a week after Yugoslavia had been forced to capitulate Greece too was conquered; and by the end of April Hitler could – and did – taunt his generals with their apprehensions and point with triumph at

t: General Erwin Rommel. *Above:*
...tonescu (right) the Rumanian Prime
...nister listens as his country is made a
...rman puppet state, December 1941

...o entire nations brought to heel
...hin a month in a campaign for
...ich no-one had the stomach'.

...Nothing could have been more
...ent fuel for his blazing megalo-
...nia. Metaphorically rubbing his
...ds with the glee of the general for
...om no world is too great to conquer,
... campaign to complex, he ordered
... re-timed start of 'Barbarossa'.
...e offensive was to begin at 0330 on
...d June, and the codeword 'to set
...ssia aflame and cause the world to
...d its breath' was 'Dortmund'.

...recisely on its scheduled hour
... codeword was given and the three
...ny groups began 'Barbarossa'. Two
...rs later the German Ambassador
...Moscow called on Molotov and told
...n Germany had decided to attack
...ssia because too many Red Army
...ops were in evidence along
... frontier and were threatening
...rmany 'in defiance of the Pact of

22nd August 1939'. In Germany, at
seven o'clock, Goebbels broadcast the
Führer's proclamation, which in tone
was that of a shining Crusader in pur-
suit of a particularly noxious dragon:

'Weighted down with heavy cares,
condemned to months of silence, I
can at last speak freely. German
people! At this moment a march is
taking place that, for its extent,
compares with the greatest the world
has ever seen. I have decided again
today to place the fate and future of
the Reich and our people in the hands
of our soldiers. May God aid us,
especially in this fight.'

This nauseating bit of self-righteous
insolence was answered the same day
by Churchill in a broadcast that
edged round the difficult corners of a
policy that up to now had treated
Russia as hand-in-glove with Hitler
and therefore equally intolerable. It
too had its nauseous moments:

'The past, with its crimes, its follies,
its tragedies, flashes away. I see the
Russian soldiers standing on the
threshold of their native land, guarding the fields which their fathers have

113

Halder, Army Chief of Staff

tilled from time immemorial. I see them guarding their homes where mothers and wives pray – ah, yes, for there are times when all pray – for the safety of their loved ones, the return of the breadwinner, of their champion, their protector. I see the ten thousand villages of Russia . . . where there are still primordial human joys, where maidens laugh and children play'.

This roseate vision, though emotionally on key for the occasion for which it was written, like most of Churchill's speeches, was far from accurate. There were no Russian soldiers standing on the threshold guarding the tilled fields or the praying wives and mothers. 'The frontier guards, awakened by the squeal and clatter of tank tracks, were shot down as they emerged from their barracks, running half dressed through the smoke', says Alan Clark in *Barbarossa*. Aircraft were bombed to destruction as they stood on the airfields, as had happened in Poland. There was virtually no organized resistance against the tremendous impact of the initial invasion. For many days the Germans drove on into Russia almost unopposed. There were vast defensive forces but no plans. Heroic battles were reduced to mere skirmishes for lack of direction. Within a month Hitler's armies had

overrun three hundred miles on t whole of the thousand-mile front fr Finland to the Black Sea.

On 3rd October he broadcast himse 'I declare today – and I declare without any reservation – that t enemy in the East has been stru down and will never rise again.'

It was characteristic of him that soon as flaws appeared in the structure of his enterprises he plastered the over with the reassurances of a m pretending that unexpected ever have been anticipated.

The first flaw had begun to appear August. It was rather more than hairline in the outer surface of t relationship between Hitler and t generals – always very thin ice. T problem, as always, was one strategy – the generals clinging to t orthodox, Hitler to what he saw bold and definitive.

Broadly, Hitler had determined the plan outlined in the directi in the north to clear the Baltic Stat and capture Leningrad with the of Army Group Centre; in the south press toward Kiev and the Dniepr a lay hold of the vast resources of t Ukraine.

The generals, disturbed by t sudden stiffening resistance of the R Army and the thinness of the Germ line caused by its excessive leng had different ideas. 'We have und estimated Russia', Halder reported 17th August. 'We reckoned with divisions and we have already iden fied 360. We have no depth in c offensive line and in consequence t enemy counter-attacks often me with success.'

He and Brauchitsch pressed for concentrated attack on Mosco Hitler, however, would have none of 'He has rejected the Moscow pla Halder wrote in his diary, 'and h decided that the strongest possi forces from Army Groups Centre a South are to be concentrated for great pincer movement against t Soviet forces east of Kiev. The aim defeating decisively the Russi

mies in front of Moscow has been
bordinated to the desire to obtain
e Ukraine . . . But the Führer has
so now become obsessed with the
ea of capturing both Leningrad and
alingrad, for he has persuaded him-
lf that if these two holy cities of
mmunism fall, Russia will collapse'.
The Kiev pincer movement was not
mpleted until 20th September, by
ich time it was becoming clear that
e blitzkrieg techniques that worked
well in the West quickly lost
mentum in the vast steppes of
ssia and eroded the German forces
vay in impossibly long lines of
mmunication and difficulties of
rrain. Hitler, however, drunk now
th the false power of self-conviction,
imed in a scene of demonic triumph
at his forces had won 'the greatest
ttle in the history of the world'.
lder dryly noted in his diary that in
s opinion 'it was the greatest blunder
the Eastern campaign; for in the six
eks between the fall of Smolensk
d the taking of Kiev the opportunity
seizing Moscow was lost.'
Since this was the point at which we

**Brauchitsch (left) and Halder
were unable, after 1940, to stand up to
Hitler**

see in retrospect the beginning of the
end for Germany and the trail of
Hitler's footsteps starting their rapid
descent from the crest of power to the
depths of ignominy, the moment is
convenient to examine and label the
seeds of defeat.

First and most disastrous was his
insane determination to crush Yugoslavia without mercy and thereby
delay the start of 'Barbarossa' by five
fateful weeks. In his rage at Yugoslavia's refusal to acquiesce to the
pact-signing grovelling of the puppet
Regent, Hitler had deflected the course
of action from that laid down in his
own directive: 'The Russian winter is
. . . a deciding factor. The victory must
must be completed before we are
called upon to fight the weather. All
my plans are determined by that
factor.' That was wise. But it was
idiocy unbounded suddenly and solely
for spite to increase a hundredfold
the risk of encounter with the grim

Above: The Balkan Campaign, April 1941. A pontoon bridge hastily built over the River Vardar in Southern Yugoslavia. *Below:* Barbarossa. A supply column move down a road in North Russia

Barbarossa. The pace slackens. *Above:* Exhausted infantrymen rest against a tank
Below: By October 1941 winter had begun. For the Germans the going became even tougher

Barbarossa assault

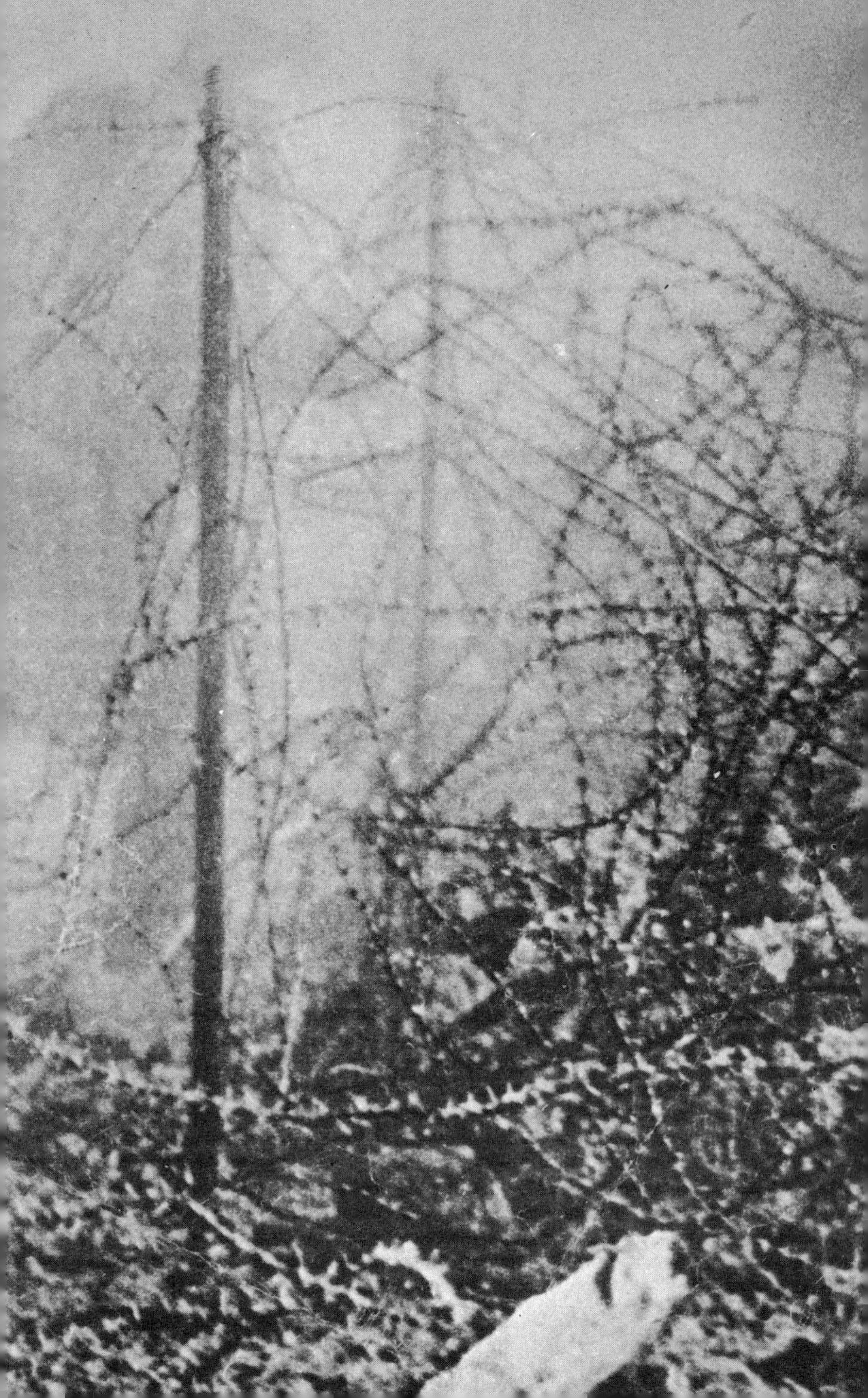

adversary of Napoleon, having already acknowledged the necessity of avoiding it.

Further delay had been caused by the profitless efforts of Halder and Brauchitsch, and the Army commanders, to persuade Hitler to change his mind. All in all, two months had been wasted.

There had been no misapprehension on Hitler's part regarding one side of the Russian character. 'The Russian will fight to the death on any given piece of ground; he will not yield it; you must destroy him.' But his contempt for their disorganization was to some extent misplaced. Lessons had been learned in Finland. The startling speed with which, once the tremendous advance into Russia had been made, the invaders were counter-attacked was dangerously effective on such a wide front; and although some half a million Russians had been trapped in the Kiev pincers, plus another alleged half million in a subsequent encircling movement at Vyazama, the tremendous effort had wearied the Germans at the very moment when they needed fresh impetus to attack across terrain turned into a quagmire by early rains.

His obsessive determination to see Stalingrad and Leningrad fall cost him vast numbers of men and machines. Indeed the battle for Stalingrad proved to be the longest battle of the war – it lasted six months – and the complete end of the German Sixth Army; while the siege of Leningrad, during which countless thousands of Leningraders died of starvation, exhaustion and cold, yet held their beleagured city against the enemy for nine hundred days, proved another facet of the Russian character that Hitler had underestimated – endurance. (The full stories of both cities in World War Two are told in *Stalingrad: The turning point* and *The Siege of Leningrad*, Battle Books 3 and 5 in this series.)

His contempt for his generals' judgement also, in the Eastern Campaign, reached maniacal proportions. The ludicrous result was that he gradually extended his insidious power downward until he literally could, and often did, control the movement of formations no larger than infantry platoons. Liddell Hart says that Rundstedt told him that toward the end of the war 'the only troops I was allowed to move were the guards in front of my own headquarters'.

The ambience of the daily 'conferences' he held is confirmed by many of the senior officers who gave evidence at the post-war Nuremberg trials. It was in every way similar to the imaginative constructions of those novelists given to building their melodramas round the efforts of power maniacs to gain control of the world.

'The reports of field commanders, collected and summarized by senior officers, would be given to him and he would direct the movement of this or that brigade or battalion, turning to the large-scale and highly detailed maps that were always the pictorial focal point of the conferences. His fantastic memory for detail often made him demand to know what had happened to, say, a particular machine-gun post. Why if its gunner had been killed, there had not been another at hand to take his place and "kill more enemy". When he was told once that "troops simply do not hold their ground when it's twenty-two degrees below zero" he gave orders that the post commander was to be shot immediately'.

His ravings were emphasized by bouts of uncontrollable twitching and sweating, moments when he was doubled up with obvious stomach pains, and an increasing tendency to wilful deafness when he was told of some indisputable fact that caught him momentarily at a loss to defend one of his own errors of judgement.

'Every midday conference became an absolute ordeal for the General Staff. The Führer would often either be screaming with frenzy or collapsing

to a chair to become consumed with
lf-pity in which every reverse was
used by disloyalty or the weakness
d stupidity of his allies. There were
course long spells of lucidity too,
d in these his brilliance as a com-
ander of every kind of formation was
quently evident. The trouble was,
at in his position as supreme com-
ander he should long ago have ceased
concern himself with the movement
patrols; but he could not bear to let
ntrol of anything pass from his
nds. He was convinced he was super-
man and that the great destiny he
rved would transcend all perils and
erything be brought to a trium-
ant conclusion.'

Triumphant conclusions were, as we
ow, far from the intention of his
stiny; and avoidance of the *Tabes
rsalis* that forced him toward general
ralysis of the insane was now
possible. *Tabes dorsalis* or *Locomotor
ixia*: syphilis involving the posterior
lumns of the spinal cord, is charac-
rized by paroxysms, functional dis-
ders of the stomach, inco-ordination
voluntary movements, and distur-
nces of vision. The infecting orga-
m *Spirochaeta pallida* that had

enlarged his natural egotism into a
state that grasped at, and to a great
extent achieved, the absolute power of
the megalomaniac, now had him in its
absolute power. Lord Acton's gnomic
dictum might be ironically adapted as
'All power corrupts and syphilitic
power corrupts absolutely'.

Those, then, were the seeds of
Hitler's and Germany's defeat. The
generals had always been apprehensive
about war on more than one front.
Africa, the Balkans, the Atlantic,
the Mediterranean – there was, as
Westphal pointed out, a limit to the
manpower and productive capacity
of every nation. No-one could deny
the Führer's skill in launching and
carrying to success so much in so
short a time. (The speed of that
success had been largely due to the
long and careful political preparation
during the years 1919 to 1939.) No-one
could deny either his almost visionary
insight into the reactions of his
opponents, military and political. But
certainly no-one could deny his madness in refusing, as the Russian

**Destroyed and abandoned German
equipment lines a road outside Moscow**

ft: **Bormann, still in the side-lines**
a **Party-rally planning conference in**
34. *Above:* **With Keitel and Hitler at**
hrerhauptquartier **in 1941**

mpaign dragged wearily on, to
cept any of the strategic plans of
e men on the spot; for they were
ins that could have ended, at best,
ly in negotiation or compromise.
d nothing would have induced him
accept such a solution. As Chester
lmot comments in *The Struggle*
Europe:
He knew that neither his personal
wer nor that of the Nazi Reich
uld survive a settlement by
gotiation. Having submitted the
ture of his régime, and of Germany,
the gamble of war, he had to
ntinue to the last throw in the hope
at the winning numbers would
rn up. Total Victory or Total
feat: that was the essence of the
hilist philosophy which was the
ndation of Nazism.'
Dressed up, of course, it sounded
ce a brave man's clarion call. It
.s a call he had trumpeted a
ndred times:

'I shall strike and not capitulate.
The fate of the Reich depends on
me alone. Every hope of compromise
is childish. It is Victory or Defeat.
The question is not the fate of a
National-Socialist Germany, but who
is to dominate Europe in the future.
No one has ever achieved what I
have achieved. My life is of no importance in all this. I have led the
German people to a great height,
even if the world does hate us now.
I am setting all my achievement on a
gamble. I have to choose between
victory and destruction. I choose
victory. As long as I live I shall think
only of the victory of my people. I
shall shrink from nothing and destroy
everyone who is opposed to me. I
shall stand or fall in this struggle.
I shall never survive the defeat of my
people. There will be no capitulation
to the powers outside, no revolution
by the forces within.'

No: no-one could deny any of those
things, those facts. The generals
least of all. And perhaps many of them
remembered the phrase 'I shall never
survive the defeat of my people'.
Hitler had said it to them in 1939.

123

The General in defeat

On the very day that Hitler was gloating over the signing of the Franco-German armistice in the railway car in the Forest of Compiègne – 22nd June 1940 – the first step was being taken to regain a British foothold on the continent of Europe. It was a faltering footstep; but it denied the validity of Hitler's promise that no Anglo-Saxon should ever land on the mainland again.

On the 23rd, at Churchill's instigation, a hundred commandos in a couple of boats – all that could be spared – made a raid on the French coast near Boulogne. Their object was to bring back prisoners and information about the coast defences there. They were unsuccessful; and indeed some of them, navigating themselves to the wrong port on their return journey, were ignominiously hauled ashore by the Military Police and arrested for desertion.

It was a brave if farcical beginning to the immense operation 'Overlord' that on 6th June 1944 brought the war in Europe to its final battles; but it

served to convince Churchill and t Army Command that though Brita was at that time helpless in terms men and weapons sight must never lost of the necessity for an eventu full-scale invasion. The convicti determined Churchill to form a Co bined Operations Command who task was to study and report on eve possibility of achieving that obje

It was clear to anybody capable making a simple statistical calcu tion that only the withdrawal of t bulk of the German occupation forc in north-west Europe could make invasion possible. And at that tin with Hitler's men in gleeful possessi of France and the Low Countri and German headquarters establish triumphantly in fallen Paris, t likelihood of a withdrawal for a reason was, as the Chief of t Imperial General Staff recorded wi

20th July 1944. Hitler, his hand bandaged, with Bormann, Jodl (bandaged head) and underlings soon after the bomb attempt

Joseph Stalin

masterly understatement, 'somewhat remote'.

Remote it remained, until precisely one year later and the start of 'Barbarossa'. The Battle of Britain and the increasing intensity of the Battle of the Atlantic fully occupied the attentions of the navy and the air force; and the army was desperately trying to overcome its decimation in France by training the thousands of conscripts who were gradually being drained from civilian life and for whom there seemed to be a permanent shortage of weapons and equipment. Then, with Russia betrayed in June 1941 – partly through her own greed and stupidity in allying herself with Germany – the balance of power shifted. It was a slight shift indeed: Hitler still kept fifty divisions defending northwest Europe and Norway. But it became evident as 'Barbarossa' progressed that the huge numbers needed to maintain the momentum of the invading forces must eventually be replenished from Europe or Africa.

Stalin, with a grizzling petulance discreditable in the leader of a great nation, did not fail to draw what he thought were the obvious deductions: that Britain should at once create a second front in Europe and so necess tate the return of some of the 1! German divisions engaged on t Eastern Front. His correspondent with Churchill at this time is full accusations, appeals and demand 'It was British failure in France th enabled Germany to invade t Ukraine . . . The Germans consid that England is merely bluffing, a they laugh at her cowardice whi they transfer division after divisio to the East where our people sp their blood in defending our lar against the growing might of t Nazis . . . Only when Britain opens Second Front can we be assured of h friendship . . . How soon will aid con from Britain?'

With admirable restraint Churchi refrained from 'rubbing salt trut into the Russian wounds'. Americ called by her President 'the gre arsenal of democracy', had by th time under Lease-Lend begun suppl ing Britain with arms and armou ships and ammunition. Many of the supplies, though sorely needed in t battles against Rommel in Africa a for equipping the expanding arn in Britain were being divert to Russia; and Churchill insi tently maintained, with considerab patience and dignity in his repli to Stalin, that that was all that cou be done for the moment – 'thou I have already agreed with Preside Roosevelt that one of our princip aims should be to go to the aid of t conquered populations by landi armies of liberation when the oppc tunity is ripe'.

The opportunity was of cour advanced by the Japanese attack Pearl Harbor on 7th December 19 At once America toppled over t brink of a neutrality sympathetic Allied causes into unremitting w Two weeks later Churchill, Roosev and George C Marshall (Chairman the US Joint Chiefs of Staff) met Washington and agreed on 'the st tegic direction of all the forces both nations, the allocation of m

wer and munitions, the co-
dination of communications, the
ntrol of military intelligence, and
e joint administration of captured
eas'. It was also agreed that,' not-
thstanding the entry of Japan into
e war, our view is that Germany
still the prime enemy and her
feat is the key to victory. Once
ermany is defeated, the collapse
Italy and the defeat of Japan
ust follow.'
Firm words. And indeed their
eaning and the consequent intention
ver wavered. But they were put
mewhat awry by the lightning
eed of events in the Far East.
ngapore fell to the Japanese
vaders on 15th February 1942 and
ere ensued a grave threat that the
xis powers might link up in the
dian Ocean, thus at one stroke
olating India, endangering Austra-
sia, and leaving Russia's eastern
aboard vulnerable. To combat this
reat it was necessary to divert the
ain Allied effort to halting the
Japanese and safeguarding the Persian
oilfields. No immediate concentration
on the invasion of Europe was therefore possible.

There were in fact to be many more
delays. These were caused mainly by
the immense shipping losses in the
Battle of the Atlantic, the continuing
urgent demands by Russia for equipment for the desperate battles that
raged month after month, and the
incessant endeavour to build up the
forces needed to defeat Rommel in the
desert. Against these demands it was
impossible to build up the equally
necessary power to ensure success in
a continental invasion. All the Chiefs
of Staff were agreed that to attempt
the invasion with inadequate forces
would be to invite disaster. Stalin's
petulance had turned to a somewhat
threatening belligerence; and he
secured from Roosevelt an unwisely

'The Anglo-Saxons'. Roosevelt and
Churchill at their Atlantic meeting,
August 1941. General Marshall on left

In the bag. General von Arnim surrenders to the British, Tunisia 1943

given undertaking that the Second Front invasion would be carried out in the second half of 1942. This communiqué was immediately qualified by Churchill in a note that said categorically 'It is impossible to say in advance whether the situation will be such as to make this operation feasible when the time comes. We can therefore give no promise in the matter.' But the Russians had already published the communiqué and for many months its promise proved embarrassing to the Allies and aroused considerable anger in Britain, where there was a characteristic feeling that promises should be honoured, not qualified.

Hitler, in his monstrous arrogance, appears to have convinced himself that so long as he kept up the war on shipping it would never be possible for the Allies to mount an invasion. In one of his frenzies he shouted at Field-Marshal Paulus, commander of the German Sixth Army in Russi[a] that 'neither England nor Ameri[ca] singly or together can outdo [us] in military genius – and it is tha[t] not mere numbers, that always d[e]cides victories'.

All the same, he spared no numbe[r] in ordering a new offensive in t[he] Stalingrad sector in October 1942 a[nd] another in the south. Both these ca[me] to grief by the massive counter-atta[ck] launched by Marshal Timoshenko [on] 19th November 1942. By 31st Janua[ry] 1943 Paulus had been forced to surre[n]der. All available reinforcing Germ[an] troops were sent forward from t[he] Caucasus; but the Russians too h[ad] some strategic ability if not geni[us.] The German move had been antic[i]pated and the reinforcements we[re] cornered. If 'Barbarossa' as a ca[m]paign had been the decisive point [at] which Hitler turned toward defe[at,] Timoshenko's counter-offensive w[as] the pivot on which the ultima[te] German retreat was balanced. Aft[er] it, battles flared up, offensives a[nd] counter-offensives were mounte[d]

128

lifference into hopeless attacks and
few of these gained ground, or re-
ined that which had been lost, for
tler. But it had become apparent
en to him that the tide had turned
the Allies. He may well have fol-
wed Clausewitz' dictum: 'He who
es force unsparingly without refer-
ce to the bloodshed involved, must
tain a superiority if his adversary
es less vigour in its application.' But
s adversary in this case unexpec-
lly followed the same dictum – and
ed more vigour.

Also using more vigour – or more
nning strategy – was General Mont-
mery in Africa, his opponent-in-
ief being General von Arnim, who
d replaced Rommel in Tunisia.
ere the final battles in the African
mpaign raged until 12th May 1943,
en Arnim surrendered. 'The North
rica Campaign had reached its
nclusion', says Montgomery, 'and
e remaining Axis survivors were
lged in captivity. It had ended in a
ajor disaster for the Germans; all
eir remaining troops, equipment
d stores were captured. Very few
rsonnel were able to get away
ving to the effectiveness of the
ockade by the Royal Navy and Royal
r Force which closed the escape
utes by sea and air. It is idle to
eculate why the Axis forces at-
mpted to hold on in North Africa . . .
om a purely military point of view
ere was no justification for their
tion, but perhaps there were over-
ding political considerations.'.

The 'political considerations' were
more than Hitler's involvement
th his Axis partner, who had proved
be a broken reed. A much more
sistent consideration was his own
fusal to believe that anything he
rected could possibly go wrong.
roughout the war his generals
tempted to persuade him to
rrender when surrender was justi-
d – as it must sometimes be in war –
d thereby gain advantage for the

The invasion of Italy. Salerno beach,
September 1943

The invasion of France. A mass of US equipment on the beach, Normandy, June 1944

above: Rundstedt, Commander in
the West. Hitler undermined his
authority by giving Rommel command
of the troops in France, and then, on
1st July 1944, replaced him by Kluge
left: General Kluge

...ture; and even more often they had
...ied to dissuade him from what
...eemed to them sheer madness in
...ilitary tactics – as for example in his
...retended intention to invade France
...mmediately on the outbreak of war
...1939. In that and other cases they
...ad been proved wrong and had reaped
...itler's taunts. His generalship had
...ot been entirely undermined by his
...ania for individual power until he
...w Russia within his grasp; and even
...en he might have come to conquest,
...r at any rate there might have been a
...ery different outcome on the Eastern
Front, if he had not allowed his
vicious attack on Yugoslavia to delay
the opening of 'Barbarossa' by those
fateful five weeks.

As things were now, in 1943, he was
soon to find his armies retreating on
all fronts. The invasion of Sicily began
on 10th July and was completed by
17th August. It was called by Montgomery, whose Eighth Army, together
with the Seventh US Army carried out
the operation, 'the first strike at the
soft underbelly of the Axis in Europe'.
It was a successful strike not only in a
military sense but as a political move
also Mussolini, brought time and
again to impotent rage by his failure
to influence Hitler, and to ignominy
by the feeble performances of his
swaggering, windfilled troops, was
beside himself with fury at this new
insult to Fascism. His son-in-law,

The scene at Rastenberg after the failure of Struffenberg's attempt. *Above:* Keitel, Göring, Hitler, and Bormann; Himmler behind. *Below:* The Duce is suitably moved by Hitler's escape

Count Ciano, says that he began to issue orders and counter-orders 'in a sequence that could lead only to certainty of his further inability to lead the country'. On 25th July, by which time the German defenders of the island had been forced back by the Seventh US Army to the north coast, the Italian dictator resigned and was immediately put under arrest by his successor, Marshal Badoglio. Badoglio entered into secret negotiations with the Allies and on 3rd September, when the Eighth Army was crossing the Messina Strait to land on the toe of Italy, signed an armistice treaty and agreed that it should be kept secret until Allied landings had been made at Salerno. The landings were made a few days later (on the 8th) and the news of the Italian capitulation broadcast.

Fortunately for Hitler the Allies did not follow up the Salerno landing either quickly or effectively – a failure for which the Supreme Commander, Eisenhower, later came in for considerable criticism. That failure allowed Hitler to demonstrate delaying action in Italy; indeed the final surrender of all German troops in Italy did not take place until 29th April 1945. But the delay did not alter the fact that once the Allies had secured their foothold in Sicily Hitler's armies were doomed – not least because that and earlier co-ordinated amphibious operations, of which the first was the tiny Commando raid of 2nd June 1940, had brought to the Combined Operations Command a wealth of experience that was to accumulate into the know-how for launching the greatest amphibious operation of all time – 'Overlord'.

At Soissons, only twenty miles east of Compiègne, there was an elaborate concrete bomb-proof shelter which Hitler had had built for his headquarters for the 'Sea Lion' operation in 1940. At nine o'clock on the morning of 17th June 1944 he arrived here for a meeting with his generals. Rommel and Rundstedt were there, and the scene was recorded by General Hans Speidel:

'He looked pale and sleepless, playing nervously with his glasses and an array of coloured pencils which he held between his fingers. He sat hunched upon a stool, while the Field-Marshals stood. His hypnotic powers seemed to have waned. There was a curt and frosty greeting from him. Then in a loud voice he spoke bitterly of his displeasure at the success of the Allied landings, for which he tried to hold the field commanders responsible. The meeting lasted until four o'clock. At midday Hitler bolted a heaped plate of rice and vegetables after it had been previously tasted for him. Pills and liqueur glasses containing various medicines were ranged round his place and he took them in turn. Two SS men stood guard beside his chair.'

Everything here is indicative of the character of the man and the state of his health and mind. The crude ranting and transference of blame from his own shoulders to those of the professionals he hated; the hypochondria; the fear that comes to all megalomaniacs that brooding conspiracies exist (it was a well grounded fear, as we shall see); and the obvious, if temporary, implicit inability to deal with an overwhelming situation.

The situation did indeed demand rather more than the attention of a sick syphilitic verging on the borders of lunacy.

At 6.30 am on 6th June the first wave of five invading British and American divisions, carried in 4,266 ships and landing craft, had landed on the Normandy beaches. They had been preceded, at 2am, by more than 3,000 aircraft carrying airborne troops; an aerial bombardment from 2,219 bombers starting at 3.14am; and a naval bombardment at 5.50am. Convoying and covering the landings was a total of 702 warships and 25 flotillas of minesweepers; and in the air a total of 171 squadrons had prepared the way before D-day by

attacking railways, bridges and aerodromes. This immense force was under the Supreme Command of General Dwight Eisenhower.

In terms of men on the ground opposing it there was a much mightier force: fifty infantry and ten panzer divisions. But these of course covered a huge area – Normandy, Brittany, the Pas de Calais, Flanders, Holland, the Biscay coast and the Riviera. In Normandy were nine infantry divisions and one Panzer division. In charge and directing this defensive force – as much as any of Hitler's generals could ever be said to be directing anything – was Field-Marshal von Rundstedt, Commander-in-Chief in the West. But because he had expressed the view to Hitler that France should be evacuated and its garrison withdrawn to the German frontier, in preparation for the Allied invasion that was obviously being planned, Hitler had humiliated him by giving ostensible command of all troops in France to Field-Marshal Rommel. 'In this way', General Speidel says, 'he maliciously set the two Field-Marshals against each other, knowing that even in the *method* of defending France they had divergent views. Thus they would have to rely on him for the solution, thereby emphasizing their reliance on him.'

Having been forced to accept the decision that there would be no withdrawal to the German frontier, Rundstedt held that if France were to be defended the best method was to keep the main body of the army well back from the coast, allow the Allied force to gain a foothold, and then attack from well in the rear of the coastal defences with such power that would drive the enemy back into the sea. Rommel was all for destroying the enemy as he landed, for which he

Above: Destruction in the Falaise pocket.
Left: The Ardennes counterattack. Germans advance past abandoned US vehicles. December 1944

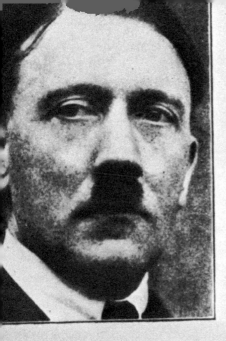

1925

1926

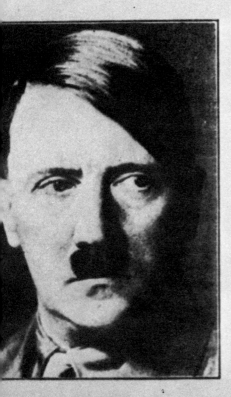

1927

1928

would naturally demand extremely strong beach garrisons backed by solidly packed reserves no more than a few miles from the coast.

The solution as given by Hitler – a fatal one – was a compromise. It was not, on the face of things, an unreasonable one. The infantry were to be kept well forward and the mechanized forces in the rear. But compromises are rarely satisfactory in desperate times; and this occasion proved to be no exception to the rule. The fact that the great warlord was supposedly directing the entire enter-

prise from his eyrie in Wolfescha[...] was of no help to anybody; while [...] maniacal order that no reserves w[...] to be thrown into the battle with[...] his personal approval was a hindra[...] that had disastrous consequences.

However, in one of his latterly r[...] flashes of psychological insight [...] proved his generalship once aga[...] and almost for the last time – that l[...] time was to be in the Ardennes in [...] coming winter – by assessing correc[...] the point at which the invasion wo[...] be made. Rundstedt had supposed [...] invasion fleet would land at [...]

Nuremberg, scene of Hitler's triumphs, falls to the Americans, April 1945

rrowest part of the English Channel, tween Calais and Dieppe, that being e method that hidebound strategy uld dictate; but Hitler, according General Warlimont, who was on staff, did not think that Eisen- wer – in no sense an orthodox eral – would concede anything to hodoxy. It was much more bable, Hitler said, that the landing if it isn't all a gigantic bluff' – uld take place between Caen and erbourg, 'because they will need a port, and what other is there?' mmel accordingly tightened up his

defences in the Normandy area.

But to be right in a psychological appreciation is of little use if one is to be wildly wrong in the administra- tion of the steps taken to meet it. To act the puppet master in a remote lair in Berchtesgaden and then to restrict one's generals in their execu- tive power is to court disaster.

The first of the disastrous con- sequences occurred before D-day. Rommel had only one Panzer division

in Normandy, and this he had positioned at Caen. Having come round – indeed not having much choice – to Hitler's viewpoint on the place of the expected landings he had asked for another Panzer division to place near St Lô – where in fact it would have been of great value in dealing with the Americans. But he was refused. Hitler having compromised on the method of defence was determined to keep his armour to the rear, and the nearest available additional armour was some miles to the north-west of Paris. This bothered Rommel so much that he determined to make a trip to Hitler's headquarters to try to persuade him. Since Hitler had forbidden his commanders to travel by air because of the activities of the Royal Air Force, Rommel made the trip by road on 5th June. He had been assured by the meteorological report that high winds and rough seas made any kind of invasion extremely unlikely. (Eisenhower had actually postponed D-day from 5th June to 6th June for that very reason.) He therefore drove first to his home near Ulm to greet his wife on her birthday and stayed with her that night. When, on the morning of the 6th he set out for Berchtesgaden the invasion had already begun.

It was therefore Rundstedt's headquarters that telephoned Hitler at 4am, as soon as the airborne landings made it virtually certain that the invasion was about to begin. They received a dusty answer. Hitler was still in bed and Jodl dared not wake him. He categorically refused to release the reserve Panzer Corps. He was certain that the Normandy landings were no more than a feint and that in a short while there would be a full-scale landing east of the Seine – 'when the reserve Panzer Corps will serve the proper purpose the Führer has decided for it'.

Meanwhile, as plea after plea was made and refused, the Americans had

Soviet bombers over Berlin, April 1945

A dishevelled-looking Führer inspects
Hitler Youth members in the garden of
the Reich Chancellery. Taken late in
March 1945, and one of the last pictures
of Hitler

got a footing on two beaches and the
British on one and in parts had
penetrated inland for five miles.
From then on the invasion was
scarcely ever to be checked.

It was scarcely surprising, therefore,
that on the morning of 17th June
Hitler should speak bitterly 'of his
displeasure at the success of the
Allied landings'. By that time the
advance had secured the link-up of
all the beach-heads into a continuous

front. 400,000 men, 60,000 vehicles, a
100,000 tons of stores had been land
The prefabricated ports called 'M
berries' had been towed across t
Channel and built and the 'Plu
(Pipe Line Under The Ocean) conti
uous oil supply laid. Air mastery w
absolute. 'In fine weather', sa
Eisenhower, 'all enemy movement w
brought to a standstill by day.'

Blind to the hopelessness of t
situation, which Rundstedt a
Rommel attempted to reveal to hi
Hitler did nothing but shriek 'The
must be no withdrawal! You mu
stay where you are!' Rundstedt ad
'He would not even agree to allow
any more freedom than before

where the Allies and their supplies continued to pour in. Needless to say, the implied criticism did nothing but arouse a towering rage in the Führer. The only thing that calmed him was a suggestion by Rommel that he should visit the Normandy battlefield and personally inspire the troops to die where they stood rather than withdraw. This he agreed to do two days hence, on the 19th.

He never made the visit. Early in the evening of the 17th, when the 'conference' with the generals had ended and Hitler was being driven to Compiègne, where presumably he intended to make some symbolic genuflection or draw some kind of inspiration, a V1 on its way to London cut its engine and fell with destructive force on the Soissons bomb shelter. No-one was hurt, but Hitler was so alarmed by his narrow escape that he turned tail and drove back to Berchtesgaden with all speed. It was an echo of his speedy disappearance from the scene of the *putsch* of 9th November 1923.

On 20th June a violent new offensive by the Russians began. It destroyed all German resistance in its path and in two weeks the eastern border of Poland had been crossed and East Prussia itself was in danger. There was nothing to be done except withdraw reinforcements from the Western Front – hardly helpful in stemming the invasion tide there. Nor was it any solution to get rid of Rundstedt – which Hitler did on 1st July because Rundstedt had expressed 'defeatist views' – and replace him by Field-Marshal von Kluge.

Nothing whatever, in fact, could now alter the course of defeat except a miracle. Hitler's generals did not believe in miracles any more than they now believed in the Führer's ability to lead Germany anywhere but into utter destruction. Though he had inspired violent personal hatred in many of the professionals for whom he had shown such contempt it was, to do them justice, not so

oving the forces as we thought best. s he would not modify his orders, e troops had to continue clinging to their cracking line. There was plan any longer. We were merely ying, without hope, to comply with itler's order that the line Caen-vranches must be held at all costs.' The only compensation he offered e generals was the new weapon, the 1 Flying Bomb, 'which it is certain ill have a decisive effect on the war , as I intend, it is directed exclusive-on London so as to bring the English the idea of peace'. Speidel says the vo field-marshals then ironically iggested that there would be more nse in directing it on to the beaches much that hatred as a wish to end the war honourably for Germany on which they based the conspiracy to kill him.

The conspiracy involved a great many people; but the actual planting of the bomb under the table in the Führer's headquarters on 20th July 1944 was done by Lieutenant-Colonel Count Klaus Schenk von Stauffenberg. Unfortunately the bomb failed to do more than inflict superficial injuries on Hitler and inspire him to tell Mussolini, whom he met an hour or so later, that divine providence had been at work again and that his life had been saved so that he in turn could save the German nation. But it led to a paralysis of fear infecting the High Command in the weeks and months that followed, for Himmler's Gestapo ruthlessly sought out all who had, or might have had, even the most tenuous association with the plot. Among them was Kluge, whose name had been found mentioned in papers revealed by the Gestapo investigation.

'All this', says Liddell Hart in *The Other Side of the Hill*, 'had a very bad effect on any chance that remained of preventing the Allies from breaking out [of the Avranches-Caen front]. In the days of crisis Field-Marshal von Kluge gave only part of his attention to what was happening at the front. He was looking back over his shoulder anxiously – toward Hitler's headquarters.'

A few days later all that was left of the defensive German armies on the Western Front became trapped in the 'Falaise Pocket'. Kluge was sacked. He committed suicide by taking a poison tablet. But it was not the humiliation of being relieved of his command that brought him to self-destruction: he had supposed – with every justification – that he would be arrested by the Gestapo within a few hours.

On 29th July General Patton's Third American Army crossed the Seine. General Eisenhower reported

that no effective barrier now l[...] between him and Brittany, for t[...] enemy was in a state of comple[...] disorganization. The invasion, [...] such, was over. According to Majo[...] General J F C Fuller, 'final victo[...] was assured irrespective of wh[...] happened on any other front. Yet [...] was more than a victory: it was [...] revolution which cracked the age-o[...] foundations of maritime securit[...] Conclusively, it showed that, grant[...] the necessary industrial and technic[...] resources, no coastline, whether of [...] continental or an insular power, ev[...] when strongly defended, was henc[...] forth secure. It proved that, h[...] Hitler allotted but a fraction of t[...]

resources at his disposal between the
years 1933 and 1939 to solving the
problem of the English Channel, he
would have won the war.'

Final victory may well have been
assured. But there was still plenty of
time for the perpetration of mistakes.
And most of them, as it happened,
were on the Allies' side. The advance
toward Germany was harried by
curious organizational failures, not
least of which was a shortage of
petrol. And in the interval, which was
accounted for by the euphemistic
phrase 'refitting, refuelling and rest',
the Germans had got together a few
weak divisions and some astonishingly
active and courageous parachutists

**Victorious Russians parade in the
shattered streets of Berlin**

who inflicted considerable damage in
spite of their small numbers. That
limited delay led to a longer one
during which a fairly stout resistance
was built up along the Rhine front. It
was a case of differing ideas of strategy
held by General Montgomery and
Generals Bradley and Patton on the
American side. Eisenhower was
naturally unwilling to approve out-
right the strategy of either the
English or American leaders and
again, with just as dire results as
Hitler had reaped, compromise was
resorted to. Here was a clash of

149

personalities that was never truly resolved, as was to be seen in the post-war memoirs of the generals concerned; and it is difficult to see what else Eisenhower could have done in the circumstances. He had become what Liddell Hart called 'the rope in a tug of war between his chief executives'.

All the same, however much blame may or may not be attached to personal antagonism in high places, the most deep-seated cause of the Allies' failure to complete their victory in September 1944 was a kind of ennui, an unjustifiably optimistic attitude of 'uh-huh! We've won the war; let's relax'. It seemed to permeate the ranks from top to bottom; and its influence reached Hitler in the form of one of his intuitive flashes of psychological insight. It was the last; but in his dying mind it inspired the boldest counterstroke of all.

On the morning of 16th December, a day after Montgomery had sent Eisenhower a cheque for £5 to settle a bet that the war would be ended by Christmas, a huge – huge considering Hitler's desperate circumstances – offensive was launched in the beautiful, hilly, wooded country of the Ardennes. This was precisely where he had launched his break-through in the spring of 1940, and it is almost unbelievable that the Allies, with everything in the history of the Second World War to prove them wrong, had ridiculously left that gate open once again – and for the same reason that France had left it open earlier: because it was considered unsuitable country for the movement of armour.

That it wasn't unsuitable was again made quickly evident. Hitler had assembled, from all he had been able to gather of his remaining tanks, plus all that had been got into production during October and November,

a new Sixth Panzer Army. Against this, stretched sparsely across the Ardennes front, were a mere four divisions. These were quickly penetrated by seven armoured and thirteen other divisions of the Sixth Panzer Army, with devastating effect. In addition, chaos was caused in the Allied lines by German commandos who, disguised in American uniforms and riding in captured American jeeps, cut communications, turned signposts, put down notices indicating non-existent minefields, and in general adapted to confusing use the technique of the Trojan Horse.

Eisenhower says that when the news of the counter-attack reached him at his headquarters at Versailles late in the afternoon of the 16th he 'was immediately convinced that this was no local attack', and he immediately alerted the two divisions he held in reserve at his headquarters. But their arrival on the scene was too late to stem the attack. Consequently the final collapse of the Reich was delayed for a little under five months – and at very great cost to the Allies, particularly the Americans, who bore the brunt of the counter-attack.

Not that the Ardennes campaign itself lasted for five months – or indeed anything like. By Christmas day Patton's Third Army had knocked the stuffing out of Sixth Panzer Army and Hitler was once more indulging in wishful thinking. 'A tremendous easing of the situation has come about', he told Rundstedt (who by that time had been reinstated in command). 'The enemy has had to abandon all his plans for attack. He has been obliged to regroup his forces. He has had to throw in again units that are tired. And at home he is being criticized and is having to admit that there is no chance of the war being decided before next August, perhaps not before the end of next year.'

Wishful thinking indeed. By 1st January Rundstedt's forces were in full retreat and by the end of

Above: This 1934 portrait shows
Hitler's fondness for dogs and the
bourgeois vulgarity of his taste. *Right:*
Posing with coalminers in the thirties

the month the total German losses
amounted to some 70,000 casualties in
men plus 50,000 prisoners, 600 tanks,
nearly 2,000 aircraft, and countless
vehicles. The Führer's intuition had
resulted in a brilliant plan; but just
as he had always built his personal
power into impossible realms of
control, so had he grossly over-
estimated his own military strength.
And though it took the Allies far
longer to recover from the shock of
his impact in the Ardennes than it
should have done, it still remained
true that final victory had been
assured when Patton's Army had
crossed the Seine and 'Overlord'
was completed.

The collapse of the Sixth Panzer
Army caused an immediate benefit
to the Russians, for on the Eastern
Front nothing could be done to keep

heir armies from advancing. And, as Major-General Fuller says, in any sane war 'hostilities would have been brought to an immediate end [after the Ardennes offensive]. But because of unconditional surrender the war was far from being sane. Gagged by his idotic slogan, the Western Allies could offer no terms, however severe. Conversely, their enemy could ask for none, however submissive. So it came about that, like Samson, Hitler was left to pull down the edifice of Central Europe upon himself, his people and their enemies. The war having been irretrievably lost, chaos was now his political aim, and thanks to unconditional surrender he was in position to achieve it.' The struggle for domination of eastern and western powers since the war is another story; but in setting in motion that struggle Hitler may be said to have achieved his aim. Which no doubt would have pleased him.

The war as a military exercise continued now in predictable leaps and bounds. Cologne was captured on 7th March, Frankfurt on the 29th, Nuremberg – where so much Nazi doctrine had been spouted and so many millions fell under the spell of Hitler's 'hypnotic personality' – on 20th April. On the 29th all German troops in Italy laid down their arms. Almost at the same moment Hitler was signing his last will in the Chancellery in Berlin while the Red Army encircled the city. It was a blindly furious document in which he attacked Jews, traitors, capitalists – even Himmler and Göring, who, he said, had betrayed him to the Allies and shamed the German nation. He denounced all who had accused him of war or warlike aims, and in what he presumably thought to be a dignified farewell, to a deeply concerned world, added:

'I cannot forsake the city which is the capital of this state. Since our forces are too small to withstand any

Hitler's public encounters with children were stage managed and publicised with great skill

...nger the enemy's attack on this ...ace, and since our own resistance ...ll be gradually worn down by an ...my of blind automata, I wish to ...are the fate that millions of others ...ve accepted and to remain here in ...e city. Further, I will not fall into ...e hands of an enemy who requires a ...w spectacle, exhibited by the Jews, ... divert hysterical masses.' (On the ...evious day Mussolini had been ...ught and executed by Italian parti-...ns while attempting to escape to ...vitzerland, and his body had been ...hibited to public insult.) 'I have ...erefore decided to remain in Berlin ...d there to choose death voluntarily ... the moment when I believe that ...e residence of the Führer can no ...nger be held.'

A few hours earlier Hitler had ...arried his mistress, Eva Braun, in a ...zarre ceremony in the bunker below ...e Chancellery. On the following day,

30th April, at 3.30 in the afternoon, Hitler took a revolver and shot himself through the mouth, and either immediately before or immediately after that suicidal shot Eva Braun swallowed poison. Hitler's body was wrapped in a blanket by Heinz Linge, his valet, and together with that of Eva Braun was soaked in petrol and burnt in the Chancellery garden. 'The sight of Hitler's shattered head', said one of the Chancellery guards who witnessed the funeral pyre, 'was repulsive in the extreme.'

It was a suitably Wagnerian end to a man who believed himself to be the saviour of the German race; and no doubt had it been possible the cremation would have been accompanied by the music of *The Entry of the Gods into Valhalla*. But nothing except the sound of Russian shells bursting was to be heard. The Gethsemane of Adolf Hitler – Führer, 'noble wolf' and 'protector of the Gentiles' – was aflame amidst the forces he had loosed upon the world and upon himself.

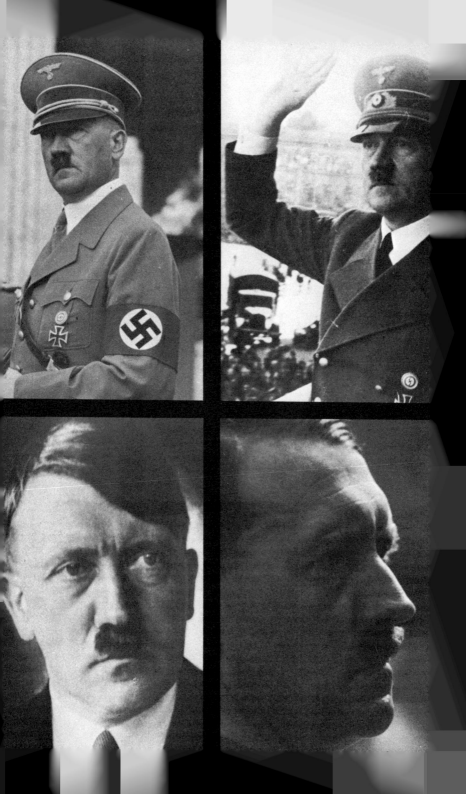

Bibliography

Hitler by Konrad Heiden (Constable)
The Last Days of Hitler by H R Trevor-Roper (Macmillan, London & USA)
Hitler's Interpreter by Paul Schmidt (Heinemann, London)
The Ciano Diaries by Count Galeazzo Ciano (Heinemann, London. Fetig, USA)
Hitler's War Directives by H R Trevor-Roper (Sidgwick & Jackson, Pan Books, London)
Inside Hitler's Headquarters by Walter Warlimont (Weidenfeld & Nicholson, London. Praeger, USA)
Hitler as War Lord by Franz Halder (Putnam)
Berlin Diary by William Shirer (Hamish Hamilton)
The Rise & Fall of the Third Reich by William Shirer (Secker & Warburg, London S & S, USA)
The Limits of Hitler's Power by Edward N Peterson (Princeton University Press USA)
The Speeches of Adolf Hitler (Oxford University Press. Fertig, USA)
Hitler by Alan Bullock (Odhams, London. Harper-Row, USA)